Contents

	Prologue	5
	Introduction	7
1	Richard Liveth Yet: 1452–1461	11
2	Royal Duke: 1461–1483	18
3	Princes in the Tower: 1483	30
4	King: 1483–1485	40
5	Henry Tudor: 1457–1485	49
6	Bosworth: August 1485	55
7	Aftermath: 1485–2012	62
8	Investigation: 2011–2013	75
9	Reburial: 2013–2014	82
	Acknowledgements	92
	Notes	92
	Bibliography	94

If we look for truth of soul, for wisdom, for loftiness of mind united with modesty, who stands before our King Richard?

Pietro Carmeliano, 1484

An homicide and murtherer of his owne bloud or progenie, an extreame destroier of his nobilitie, and to his and our countrie and the poore subiects of the same a deadlie mallet, a firie brand, and a burthen intolerable.

Raphael Holinshed, 1577

'I have set my life upon a cast, and I will stand the hazard of the die.' (King Richard)

William Shakespeare, 1592

Search, finde his name, but there is none: O Kings
Remember whence your Powre, and vastness springs:
If not as Richard now, so may you bee,
Who hath no Tombe, but Scorn and Memorie

Richard Corbett, 1647

God hath many times taken away Princes, and changed the Government of kingdoms, for the iniquities of the people; why then should not King Richard's fate be held in a modest Scale, until we can better know or judge it?

George Buck, 1674

Shakespeare's immortal scenes will exist, when such poor arguments as mine are forgotten. Richard at least will be tried and executed upon the stage, while his defence remains on some obscure shelf of the library

Horace Walpole, 1768

The Character of this Prince has been in general very severely treated by Historians, but as he was York, I am inclined to suppose him a very respectable man.

Jane Austen, c. 1790

RICHARD III

THE ROAD TO
LEICESTER

AMY LICENCE

AMBERLEY

for Tom, Rufus and Robin

Illustrations: *Previous page: Richard, Duke of Gloucester, and the Lady Anne* by Edwin Austin Abbey, courtesy of Yale University Art Gallery, Edwin Austin Abbey memorial collection. *Next page:* Courtesy of Jonathan Reeve, JR1731b90fp109C 14001500.

First published 2014

Amberley Publishing
The Hill, Stroud
Gloucestershire, GL5 4EP

www.amberley-books.com

Copyright © Amy Licence, 2014

The right of Amy Licence to be identified as the Author
of this work has been asserted in accordance with the
Copyrights, Designs and Patents Act 1988.

British Library Cataloguing in Publication Data.
A catalogue record for this book is available from the British Library.

ISBN 978 1 4456 2175 3 (paperback)
ISBN 978 1 4456 2190 6 (ebook)

Typesetting and Origination by Amberley Publishing.
Printed in Great Britain.

Prologue

22 August 1485[1]

They found him amid the marshes. He lay crumpled, encircled by the footprints of his enemies. Scavenging hands had stripped his limbs white; they lay lifeless, growing colder, streaked with blood and dirt. In the final struggle, his helmet had been cut loose, with its symbolic gold coronet. Without it, there had been little to prevent the halberds of the Welsh troops from finding their mark. The fatal blow had bitten deep into the base of the skull, yet apart from a cheek wound, his face was curiously untouched. The eyes stared up glassily into the sky, devoid of emotion, unable to see the rough hands that lifted him out of the mud.

He was thrown across the back of a horse. Someone bound his wrists – as if there was any chance that he could try and escape now! They did not attempt to cover him, laughing at his nakedness as his body lay vulnerable and exposed to the fading August sun. He was their prize now, their puppet; their jokes flew over his head as the victors began the slow tramp back into Leicester.

'Call yourself a king,' they asked, 'where is your crown now?'

Their eyes hardened in hatred and release; one spat in his direction, another drew a dagger from his belt. He was perhaps a farmer or a butcher, but for a moment, he paused, blade in hand. Some vestige of respect held him back, some sacred barrier between commoner and royalty, imbibed over centuries of feudal life. Then a primitive energy arose in his stomach, the old association of conqueror and victim, the rush of unexpected power. With a swift, low blow, the unnamed soldier thrust his knife into the flesh of the king's buttock. His companions let out a yell, half disbelief, half delight.

Someone had brought them wine. They drank it dry as they crossed back over Bow Bridge into the town, voices raised in raucous laughter. The man on the horse had lost his novelty; it went almost unnoticed when his temple struck against the stones. But word was spreading. Through the streets, people came out to watch the army pass, to see for themselves whether the rumours were true, recalling the regal figure they had seen set off for battle only forty-eight hours before. Their faces betrayed a mixture of emotions; many subdued and respectful, others relieved that it was over. Most would have wondered what the coming months and years would hold. The dead body was lain out on display, with the congealed blood about his ears already turning black; the cold earthly remnants of England's last Plantagenet king. The soldiers went away.

Two days later he was carried into the Church of the Grey Friars convent. The heavy stones in the choir had been hurriedly lifted and stacked to one side, to reveal a little space into which they would put their lord. There may have been prayers but there was little other ceremony; he was not given a shroud or a coffin. His hands were not untied. When they lifted him down, placing him on the earth, his head hung forward, jaw open. There was no time now to extend the pit, he would be buried hunched, almost sitting up in expectation. Then the slabs were replaced over his head and Richard III was consigned to history.

Introduction

2013 was Richard III's year. He scarcely needs an introduction after the way images of his cranial cavity have been broadcast into homes across the world. In the months following the discovery of his bones in a Leicester city car park, the public have learned about his diet and the condition of his teeth, the wear on his bones and the parasites swimming about in his gut. We have seen pictures of his skeleton emerging from the ground, covered in five centuries of dirt, his skull sliced and pierced, his feet victims of Victorian building works. His face has been reconstructed by layering muscles across a virtual version of his cheeks, brow and jaw. Then, the 'skin' was painted in flesh tones, a suitable wig was selected and topped with a velvet hat, replete with contemporary jewel. The great British public queued in all weathers to look into the eyes of a medieval king who was slaughtered on the battlefield. For many, it was the culmination of decades of passion and study. Centuries-old mysteries, with answers considered beyond the realms of the possible, were solved. The experience has been exhilarating, satisfying and intimate.

It has also been frustrating. For devotees of Richard, there was an excruciating wait between the reported discovery of human remains at the site in September 2012 and the DNA results five months later. But given the incredible news, the wait was well worth it. A sense of national euphoria ensured that Richard's face was unavoidable in the media, fuelling excited debate about his life and reign and spurring calls for reassessment of his reputation. Once the dust began to resettle, though, a new conflict arose. No one could have predicted just how vituperative the battle over Richard's final resting place would become. Taking various twists and turns, it developed into something more than the selection of an appropriate location, tomb and last rites. By polarising the debate between York and Leicester, something of a modern-day Wars of the Roses was enacted, prolonged by the involvement of the Plantagenet Alliance, who won the right to challenge the provision made by the university prior to their discovery.

Above left: The reconstructed head of Richard III, based on his skull, by Professor Caroline Wilkinson from the University of Dundee. (Courtesy of Victoria Munden)

Above right: An interpretation of what Richard may have looked like in life, by artist Laurie Harris. (Courtesy of Laurie Harris)

The question of Richard's reburial has become a test case about the 'ownership' or 'rights' of the living over the dead. Perhaps this should not have come as such a surprise, given that this battle has been raging in our art and literature since his death in 1485. Richard III has proved just as controversial in his cultural 'afterlife' as he was in actuality.

Soon after Shakespeare's vivid portrayal of a Machiavellian monster, a century after Bosworth, a revisionist school of thought established a Ricardian dialogue which has persisted ever since. The understandable desire to redress this cultural imbalance has not always helped the debate, though. Sometimes the late Elizabethan caricature has been replaced by an equally unrealistic alternative, fuelled by popular fiction, where a saintly Richard is absolved from any negative taint. As Simon Schama wrote in the *Financial Times* four days after the announcement of the DNA results, 'Torn between their crush and their mission of vindication, Ricardians have overcorrected, turning him into a much traduced paragon of devoted governance, personal piety.'[1] In searching for the real Richard, hagiography is as unhelpful as blame. Maintaining these positions is reductive in the attempt to rebuild a credible human being. Although the discovery of his final resting place in Leicester's Church of the Grey Friars has provided some answers, there are other mysteries that simply will never be solved.

It is the intention of this modest study to demarcate where fiction has become fact. Certain interpretations of Richard and his contemporaries have become biographical and historical memes, regurgitated through a number of works without question. This is particularly the case when it comes to the emotions and motives of people from the past, based in the assumptions of historians who are themselves a product of their own times. Quite simply, the past was another country and they did do things differently there. The quest for complete authorial objectivity is probably a misnomer though. It may even act as a barrier to logical conclusion. In spite of this, it is now essential to look at the established beliefs again, to isolate the standing stones amid the shifting sands. Somewhere amid the legend and the cultural construct, the accusations and adulation, is the real man. Part memorial, part introduction to the debate, this new guide to Richard attempts to present the facts and a few possible interpretations, to aid each reader in making up their own mind.

Richard was born at Fotheringhay Castle on 2 October 1452. Then, it would have been a formidable and large stronghold, supporting a large number of people; it was also the site of the execution of Mary, Queen of Scots, in 1587, but fell into decline after the demise of the Tudors. (Courtesy of David Noble)

Richard Liveth Yet: 1452–1461

If you visit Fotheringhay Castle today, sitting beside a bend of the River Nene, just off the A605 in Northamptonshire, you just might be disappointed. The location is pretty enough, but if you go in search of Richard III, hoping for some sort of connection with the place where he arrived into the world, you will find yourself staring up at a green mound and down at a pile of stones. Nothing else remains. You can survey the countryside from the top of the original Norman motte and get an idea why the location was considered an auspicious one in around the year 1100. And you can sense the strength of the fortifications from the densely packed knot of stones that marks the final decay of the outer wall, but the buildings that housed Richard and his family in the fifteenth century, and also witnessed the execution of Mary, Queen of Scots, in 1587, have long been demolished.

It was at Fotheringhay that Cecily Neville, Duchess of York, prepared herself to give birth during the early autumn of 1452. At the age of thirty-seven, she was relatively old to bear a child, according to the standards of the day. By this time, she had been married for over twenty years and already borne ten, perhaps eleven, children. Sadly, some of these had been lost. Infant mortality rates at the time were high but Cecily had the comfort of three surviving sons and three daughters, one of whom, Anne of York, was already married. She knew what to expect from the coming ordeal, indicated in a letter that she wrote to the queen referring to her condition as 'full painfull and unesy'.[1] Childbirth during this period was governed by superstition and religion; there was little in the way of pain relief beyond the power of prayer and many women and their babies did not survive. Even for an experienced mother like Cecily, it posed a potentially fatal risk.

Cecily's marriage appears to have been a successful one. Her husband, Richard Plantagenet, Duke of York, was an ambitious and powerful nobleman, second only to the king. His father had been executed for treason when the boy was four, but his uncle's noble death at the Battle of Agincourt the same year allowed him to inherit the title. From his mother, York inherited the Mortimer lands, the earldoms of March and Ulster and three further lordships in Ireland. The young duke's wardship had been granted to Cecily's father, the Earl of Westmorland, and he had been sent to the family home of Raby Castle, in County Durham. The pair were betrothed as children and married in their teens; the young man ambitious and driven, his new wife renowned for her beauty and piety. York's political and military career in the service of his cousin, the Lancastrian King Henry VI, had necessitated their removal to France and Ireland, but the current situation had brought them back home again.

The couple's final son, Richard, arrived on 2 October 1452. No contemporary record remains of his birth, and the date is only indicated by an entry made in a book of hours later in his life. Yet the event has become the stuff of legend. Long after his death, chroniclers and playwrights from the Tudor era exaggerated the circumstances of Cecily's delivery into the proportions of a nightmare. John Rous stretched credulity with the claim that the pregnancy had lasted two years. Thomas More added that she had 'muche a doe in her travaile'[2] and that her son arrived feet first, or breech born, with a full head of hair and the natal teeth that were considered to be signs of misfortune. Others read and repeated the story, giving it the semblance of fact. It is essential to consider the intentions and purposes of these authors, writing in the reign of Richard's nemesis, Henry VII.

Rous was the chronicler of the Neville family, into which Richard had married. He had originally been full of praise for the king, then rewrote his work after events placed him on the losing side of history. More's purpose was essentially didactic, drawing a moral lesson from those who were perceived to be villains; in turn, he had learned from those hostile to the dead king. By the time the story reached Shakespeare's hands, the precocious baby could 'gnaw a crust at two hours old'.[3] These portrayals of Richard, from a purely literary perspective, have frequently been used to fill the void of surviving evidence about the actual birth and must be recognised as part of Richard's literary 'afterlife'; the powerful legends that must be teased out from a factual narrative of events. Cecily and her new baby son came through the dangerous ordeal without any contemporary record of unusual circumstances.

Whatever the precise circumstances of his birth, the young Richard was healthy enough to survive against the considerable odds of juvenile illness and accident. In 1456, when he was four, a poet recorded his family members in the Clare Roll and described him in a way that some have taken as indicative of childhood weakness or frailty. Perhaps it was his parents' high record of infant mortality in their children that prompted the comment 'Richard liveth yet.' As a result, there

Above left: St Mary and All Saints church, Fotheringhay. It is likely that Richard was baptised in the church nearest his place of birth; a Richard Wancourt was vicar at the time. It was completed around 1434 in the Perpendicular style and became a mausoleum for the York family. Richard's father and brother Edmund were reinterred here in 1476 and his mother Cecily laid to rest in 1495. (Courtesy of Amanda Miller at Amanda's Arcadia)

Above right: Window at St Mary and All Saints church, Fotheringhay, containing Yorkist iconography, particularly the sun in splendour, the white rose, falcon and fetterlock and the boar associated with Richard himself. (Courtesy of Simon Leach)

has been further speculation that Richard was a weak or sickly child, allied with the cartoonish descriptions of him by More and Shakespeare.

It is quite likely that Richard, along with all children of the time, suffered from bouts of illness during his early years, but the discovery of his bones in September 2012 has established that he was not the caricature of legend. He did suffer from adolescent onset scoliosis, which resulted in a curved spine and affected his gait and height, although this did not develop until the age of ten at the earliest. 'Richard liveth yet' probably reflected the vulnerability of all small children given the odds of survival. The final York sibling, Ursula, was born and died in 1455, soon before the Clare Roll was composed, so the comment may simply compare that loss with her brother's endurance.

Richard spent his first years at Fotheringhay, with his mother, brother George (three years his elder), and sisters Elizabeth and Margaret. Two elder brothers, Edward and Edmund, were educated according to the practice of the time in their own establishment at Ludlow Castle. Their father, the Duke of York, was the most important magnate of the day. His presence was frequently required at the heart of government, in France or on his Irish estates. By 1452, the increasingly volatile political situation would soon propel the aristocracy into violence. Both Richard's parents claimed descent from Edward III, making their family one of the most powerful in the land, cousins to the present Lancastrian royalty. It also made them ambitious and conscious of the seniority of their claim over the current ruling house, although they had been passed over because their descent came through the female line.

York's cousin, Henry VI, was a pious and ascetic man, unsuited to kingship. As a result, his wife, Margaret of Anjou, and her favourites, the Dukes of Suffolk and Somerset, had taken an increasingly prominent role in decision making. York was particularly incensed by their handling of the recent French wars and considered Somerset to be inept, even corrupt. Suffolk's death in 1450 removed his influence; he had drowned in mysterious circumstances, having been thrown over the side of a boat, possibly on York's orders. Then, Henry VI's fragile mental health broke down completely. In 1453, he suffered a complete collapse and descended into a catatonic state, incapable of speech and unable to recognise his wife and newborn son, Edward of Westminster. Someone needed to take charge of the country until the king's wits returned. York and Somerset now both went for the reins of power but York had the senior claim. He was appointed Protector with the support of Parliament. Two years later he fought and defeated Somerset at the First Battle of St Albans. Then Henry recovered and York stepped aside.

When Richard was seven, the tide of fortune turned against his family. The Lancastrian queen, Margaret of Anjou, had never forgiven York for his attacks upon her authority. Equally, the new Duke of Somerset was keen to avenge his father's death. They assembled a 'Parliament of Devils' at Coventry in 1459, from which York and his ally Warwick were excluded, leaving them in little doubt that they were soon to be arrested. Richard was at Ludlow when the royal army approached, intent on capturing the town and defeating York. Outnumbered, his father was forced into exile in Ireland, leaving his wife and younger children behind. The duke was attainted by Parliament, declared a traitor, and his lands were seized by the Crown.

Without her husband by her side, Cecily had little choice but to submit to the rule of Henry VI and was placed in the custody of her sister Anne at Tonbridge

Micklegate Bar, York. In 1460, Richard's father, the Duke of York, and his seventeen-year-old brother, Edmund, Earl of Rutland, were killed at the Battle of Wakefield. Their heads were displayed on the gate, York's reputedly dressed in a paper crown. (Courtesy of Paul Fairbrass)

Castle in Kent. Her young children initially went with her, although Richard and George also spent some time in the household of the Archbishop of Canterbury, Thomas Bourchier, another distant cousin tracing back his line to Edward III. This situation did not last long, though. The following summer, Richard's eldest brother, Edward, accompanied by the Earl of Warwick and his father, the Earl of Salisbury, returned from their exile in Calais and captured Henry VI at the Battle of Northampton. The way was now clear for York's reunion with his family. He landed in Wales that September and Cecily travelled to meet him, leaving her children in London.

The duke was hoping to capitalise even further on the victory. With Henry VI now no more than a puppet king in Yorkist hands, he headed for Westminster and made a dramatic entrance, laying his hands on the throne and claiming his hereditary right to rule. His descent from Edward III's second son placed him in a senior line of the family to his rivals, who had usurped the legitimate succession back in 1399, although York's claim was derived through the female line. The Lancastrian Henry may have been an unwilling and inept ruler, but he was still the anointed king and had a young son and heir of his own. York's impulsive gesture caused embarrassment and inspired little support. It was far too revolutionary and unexpected and was rejected by the House of Lords. Instead, he accepted Parliament's concession that he would be named as Henry's heir and rule after his decease. This, however, disinherited the young Prince of Wales, the seven-year-old Edward of Westminster, and his mother was not prepared to stand back and allow that. The situation rapidly descended into war again, but this time, the victory went against the Yorkists. Richard was just eight when his father and brother Edmund were killed at the Battle of Wakefield in December 1460. Their severed heads were displayed on Micklegate Bar in York, dressed in paper crowns.

Panic hit London. The city feared that the queen's triumphant troops would ransack their homes, loot and pillage, as they were rumoured to have done in the North. Cecily decided that the safest place for Richard and George was in the Low Countries, so the boys set sail from England, unsure if they would ever be in a position to return. Yet their older brother was preparing to act. Although York was dead, his eldest son, the eighteen-year-old Edward, was now Earl of March and intent upon revenging his father's death and asserting his claim. Tall, athletic and handsome, he seemed everything a king should be to the medieval mind, in comparison with the ascetic Henry, who preferred not to take an active part in warfare.

Edward was an inspired military leader. Shortly before the Battle of Mortimer's Cross, he witnessed a vision of three simultaneous suns in the sky, an atmospheric

A carving of a white rose, symbol of the Yorkist dynasty, from a bridge in York. (Courtesy of Mike Smith)

Claes Visscher's view of London Bridge from 1616, including the Tower. This is the world Richard would have observed when he visited London. (Courtesy of Stephen Porter)

phenomenon known as a parhelion, or sun dog. There was an obvious symbolism in this for the House of York, who used the sun in splendour, along with the white rose, as its personal device. Fighting prominently among his troops, he went on to win a decisive victory at the Battle of Mortimer's Cross in February 1461. Edward then marched south, arriving in London before the queen's feared armies. He was welcomed by the city and was proclaimed king in March, creating the awkward situation where both York and Lancaster had laid claim to the throne. Yet the main body of Henry's armies remained undefeated. One final decisive encounter followed, at Towton, on Palm Sunday, which left tens of thousands of men dead. It has been estimated to be the worst bloodbath in English history, fought through the driving snow on fields flanked by river valleys. The defeated Henry VI and his family fled to Scotland, leaving Edward IV as the only king in England.

Royal Duke: 1461–1483

The remainder of Richard's childhood was more peaceful under his brother's reign. Returning to England, he was no longer the exiled outsider but the brother of the new king, third in line to the throne after his brother George. There was much celebration and Richard was granted the title of Duke of Gloucester and elected to the Order of the Garter. He spent more time at Westminster, at Edward's sophisticated court, as well as the family's various country seats, including Fotheringhay and Ludlow. As befitted a young man of his status, his education continued under his brother's supervision, and when George began his training as a knight at Greenwich, Richard could anticipate that he would also soon learn how to wield a sword. It was considered an essential part of a young nobleman's education and one that the adult duke would certainly need.

Then, King Edward made a decision that was to change everything. Richard was not yet twelve when it emerged that his brother had married, in secrecy. Exactly when Edward told his family is unclear but it seems likely that it was at the same time he confessed before Parliament in September 1464. He may have felt obliged to admit his actions, as discussions for a match with Bona of Savoy had progressed to the point that required a commitment, so Edward interrupted his lords, sitting at Reading Abbey, with the information that he was no longer available. Worse than this, he had kept the secret for five months already, having undergone a secret ceremony with a beautiful Lancastrian widow, Elizabeth Wydeville. She was four or five years his senior and had already borne two sons. Legend has it that they met under a great oak in Whittlebury Forest, where she waited to supplicate him for the return of her lands, but in fact, they had probably already seen each other at court. It was not the match his mother, or his cousin Warwick, had wished for. By that point though, there was little they could do about it.

Around 1465, Richard was sent north to Middleham Castle, to be trained in the chivalric arts by Warwick, whose name, Richard Neville, suggests he was also possibly the boy's godfather. There, amid the Wensleydale hills, in the castle

Above and below: Tretower Court, where life in the 1470s has been reconstructed. (Amy Licence)

Above left: Richard, Duke of York, father of Richard III. (Courtesy of David Baldwin)

Above centre: Portrait of Elizabeth Wydeville, whose secret marriage to the king was to prove more controversial than anyone could have predicted in 1483. (Amberley Archives)

Above right: Elizabeth Wydeville in her coronation robes, depicted in a manuscript owned by the Skinner's Company. (Amberley Archives)

whose towering ruins still dominate the landscape, Richard was under the same roof as his future wife, Anne, then aged nine. Records place them together in the local church, kneeling in prayer and dining at the same table at Cawood Castle, for the investiture of George Neville, Warwick's brother, as Archbishop of York. In the same year, Edward gave his new queen a lavish coronation, which followed the Burgundian formalities and etiquette he admired. She conceived her first child soon after this, early in 1466 giving birth to Elizabeth of York, the first of Edward IV's ten legitimate children.

It was around this time that Richard's scoliosis developed. Undetected when he was a child, the growth spurt of early puberty probably exacerbated the underlying condition from Richard's early teens onwards. Otherwise, accounts suggest the youthful Richard was like his father in appearance, being slight, wiry and dark haired. The Neville family chronicler, John Rous, was initially favourable to Richard, describing him in 1484 as a 'most mighty Prince' who ruled 'commendably … cherishing those who were virtuous' to the 'great laud of

This and next page: Middleham Castle, where Richard was trained in the chivalric arts by his cousin Richard Neville, Earl of Warwick. Later he married Warwick's daughter Anne and the couple made their home here, where their only son was born in the mid-1470s. (Courtesy of Paul Fairbrass)

all the people'. The line drawing that accompanies his text shows a knight holding a sword, whose limbs appear in perfect proportion, his features regular, almost beneficent. It was only later, after Richard's death, that Rous would circulate horror stories about his appearance.

Another illustration suggested as representing Richard appears in the chronicle of French writer Jean de Waurin. He would have been in his early twenties at this point and stands with his back to the artist, wearing a green hat, with his limbs well-formed, with a straight spine and even shoulders. Given what is now known about Richard's scoliosis, it is not impossible that Waurin and Rous were being diplomatic in their portrayals. They may have flattered their ruler by glossing over his impediments, or perhaps the effects of his condition were not necessarily visible at the time of writing or were hidden under clothes. Many have wondered how Richard could have worn armour and fought given the curve in his spine, estimated by Leicester University as being quite severe by the time of his death. While armour was made to measure, Richard may well have undergone certain treatments to try and improve his condition.

In the fifteenth century, scoliosis, along with all other physical abnormalities and illnesses, was believed to be caused by an imbalance in the humours. A treatment called traction was available, similar to being stretched on the rack, but was very expensive. Richard could have afforded this but there is no record or evidence that he ever underwent it. Equally he might have sought the advice of a doctor to help address the imbalance by eating certain foods and avoiding others. He also may have been given ointments and creams to rub into his spine or herbal plasters to apply to the area. The eleventh-century doctor Avicenna advised that such conditions be treated by massage, or that sufferers wear a long piece of wood or metal under their clothes in an attempt to correct the curve.[1]

The most famous, or infamous, description of Richard's appearance was not written until over a century after his death. Shakespeare's dramatic caricature of his physical deformity needs to be recognised as dramatic rhetoric, an ideological distortion. It was an essential part of the Elizabethan mentality that equated villainy with physical defects. In fact, it illuminates for us just how far history itself had been deformed. It demands to be studied not as a representation of history but as part of the history of representation. Yet, given the conventions of the era, the bard's Richard is a surprisingly charismatic, enthralling and complex figure. His confidential tone, soliloquies and asides compel an audience to engage with his journey, only to see him suffer the inevitable outcome of revenge tragedy and history. By the time the play was composed in around 1592, the tradition of the king's appearance was well established and, by 1614, it had inspired an anonymous author to produce the poem *The Ghost of Richard III*, drawing together the worst of the legends about his appearance and deeds. It survives in a single manuscript copy in the Bodleian Library:

> Hollow my cheeks, upon my brest black hayre,
> The characters of spleene and virulent deedes;
> My beetle-brow, and my fyre-cyrcled eye
> Foreshow'd me butcher in my cruelty...
> So, mountaine-like was I contract behind
> That my stretch't arms (plumpe with ambitious veines)
> Might crush all obstacles and throw them downe[2]

The contemporary chroniclers Mancini, Commines and Croyland do not mention Richard having any sort of physical abnormality. The account of Italian diplomat Mancini was openly critical of the new king; he would not have held back from unflattering physical descriptions if there were any to be made. He may not have seen Richard in person but he was well placed to record gossip from the streets of London, or from those who had. Nicolas von Popplau, a Silesian who visited court in 1484, described Richard as slim and lightly built with slender arms

A cartoon depiction of Shakespeare's Richard III character. (Courtesy of the Library of Congress)

and thighs, although he admitted the king was actually three fingers taller than himself. The Scottish Ambassador Archibald Whitelaw confirmed in the same year that Richard was small, although none seemed to doubt his strength and prowess in battle. Whitelaw added that Richard had a 'countenance worthy of the highest power and kingliness, illuminated by moral and heroic virtue'. The historian John Stowe, who was born around 1525, reputedly spoke 'with old and grave men who had often seen King Richard and they affirmed that he was ... of person and bodily shape comely enough'.[3] Just as with the rumours regarding his birth, it appears that Richard was hardly monstrous in appearance, although this has served the purposes of Tudor didacticism.

When Richard was sixteen, dissention broke out within the House of York. His mentor, Richard Neville, Earl of Warwick, resented the advancement of the queen's Wydeville relatives, whom he saw as upstarts. The earl was ambitious and shared the same royal line of descent as the Yorkist kings through the Beaufort connections of their mother, Cecily, who was his aunt. He had been humiliated when his attempts to arrange a French match for Edward were defeated. Now he hoped to marry his elder daughter Isabel to Richard's nineteen-year-old brother George, Duke of Clarence, who was second in line to the throne until Queen Elizabeth bore a son. Edward refused to sanction the match, perhaps in the belief that it would give the pair too much power but mainly because he wished to arrange a diplomatic match for his brother. Any son born to Isabel would also transfer the succession away from Edward's own line.

However, Warwick and Clarence ignored Edward's ruling and sailed to Calais. Warwick was captain of the town and had sufficient authority there to defy the king. On 11 July 1469, his seventeen-year-old daughter became Clarence's wife amid five days of celebrations designed to contrast with Edward's own secret nuptials. This was only the start of their treasonous activities. A group of Northern rebels rose against Edward IV that summer, under the lead of a mysterious figure called Robin of Redesdale. Warwick may have been working behind the scenes, sending his agents to incite revolt or at least supporting those who had grown dissatisfied with King Edward. Soon they launched a very personal attack upon him, which cut to the heart of Richard's family.

Rumours circulated that Edward himself was illegitimate, the result of an adulterous liaison between his mother and a Rouen archer named Blaybourne. The Duke of York's career had taken his family to France, where his wife, Cecily, bore two sons, Edward and Edmund, in 1442 and 1443. Given the duchess's pride and piety, along with her understanding of the importance of preserving the dynastic line and the fragility of women's reputations where their chastity was concerned, such a scenario seems unlikely. A recent attempt was made to prove Edward's illegitimacy by looking at the Rouen Cathedral records, which contain the dates of his departure from the city, and comparing them with the possible conception window. However, these fail to account for the duchess's ability to travel a relatively short distance, or the possibility of the pair meeting halfway. With at least one son dead and no male heir, the couple, already in their late twenties, would have taken opportunities to be together. The dates also allow for Cecily to have undergone a pregnancy that went two weeks over her due date. If this was the case, and a difficult labour put mother and son in danger, it would also account for Edward's hurried, low-key baptism.

The rumours served Warwick's cause, though. He was probably their instigator. According to his reasoning, Clarence was actually the rightful king and now he intended to at least ensure that a grandson of his sat on the English throne. The pair crossed the Channel and issued a manifesto of support for the Northern rebels, which outlined their intention to depose Edward and which, by comparison with Richard II and Edward II, implied his subsequent death. Richard was forced to choose between his two elder brothers but remained loyal to the Crown. It also meant distancing himself from his former mentor Warwick, and Warwick's daughter Anne. He was considered too young to fight but was active in raising troops and besieging rebel strongholds.[4] The rebellion in the North proved to be the distraction Warwick had hoped for. While Edward was away from London,

Clarence and the earl marched into London, then on to Edgecote Moor, where they defeated the reinforcement army that Edward had waiting. From there, they descended on the king's camp and took him prisoner.

Yet Warwick failed to press his advantage. Perhaps he capitulated when confronted with the reality of executing Edward. After a few months, the king was allowed to escape and returned to London. A temporary peace descended and Clarence was reconciled with his brothers. However, this did not last long and discontent was soon brewing again, with Warwick's second attempt at a rebellion meeting with disaster at the Battle of Empingham, or Losecoat field, where his men cast off their livery to avoid detection. Warwick fled for France, but his entry to Calais was barred by men loyal to the king. Isabel, Duchess of Clarence, went into labour and lost her firstborn child on board a ship – some reports claim it was a boy, others state that it was a girl. Finally, Warwick was able to sail round the north coast and land in France. There he made a deal with his former enemy Margaret of Anjou and married his younger daughter Anne to Edward of Westminster, Prince of Wales. The match was dependent upon Warwick fighting for the Lancastrian cause and represented an admission that his plans for George and Isabel had failed.

To fulfil his promise to Margaret of Anjou, Warwick returned to England in the summer of 1470. Diverting Edward to the North again, he seized control of London and released the Lancastrian Henry VI from his imprisonment in the Tower. Confused, the old king was re-crowned and displayed to the people, although in reality, Warwick was pulling the strings. Caught unawares, Edward fled to the coast, almost being drowned in a tumultuous voyage across the Wash. With Richard and Anthony Wydeville, he embarked for the Netherlands, hoping for assistance from his sister Margaret, wife of the Duke of Burgundy since 1468. It has been said that the king was in such desperation that he offered to pay the captain of a ship with the coat off his back. However, they arrived safely and, from there, gathered resources and planned their return. The political situation had changed too because shortly after their flight, Queen Elizabeth had given birth to a baby son. The future Edward V arrived on 2 November 1470, in the sanctuary at Westminster. He now stood between George and the throne.

In the spring of 1471, Edward and Richard landed at the lost port of Ravenspur on England's north-east coast with a small fleet. They marched south, building their support and reuniting with a repentant Clarence, who had been aggrieved by Warwick's scheming in favour of the Lancastrian cause. Edward was welcomed back in London. There, he met his firstborn son and namesake,

Edward IV receiving a book. He is surrounded by Richard, Duke of Gloucester (the future Richard III), Anthony Wydeville, and Elizabeth Wydeville. The child is the future Edward V. (Courtesy of Jonathan Reeve JR1580b4p582 14501500)

and the family stayed with Duchess Cecily at Baynard's Castle before Edward set off to defeat his enemies in two decisive encounters. At Barnet that April, the York brothers defeated and killed Warwick, which was probably the eighteen-year-old Richard's first taste of battle. Then they marched west to Tewkesbury, where the Lancastrian Prince of Wales launched his attempt to restore his father to the throne. Here, Richard led his troops against the Duke of Somerset, son of the man his father had killed at St Albans sixteen years earlier. Prince Edward and Somerset were killed, Queen Margaret captured and the Yorkists returned in triumph to London. That night, Henry VI was murdered in the Tower of London, probably on Edward's orders. The Lancastrian threat was over.

The second phase of Edward's reign proceeded virtually unchallenged. In the spring of 1472, Richard married Anne Neville, the teenage widow of the Prince of

Tewkesbury Abbey. In 1471, Richard returned with Edward IV from exile in the Low Countries. After defeating and killing Warwick at the Battle of Barnet, they marched west and encountered the forces of the Prince of Wales, Edward of Westminster, at Tewkesbury Abbey. The prince's death, followed by that of his father in the Tower that night, removed the Lancastrian threat and secured the throne for the Yorkists. (Courtesy of Simon Jenkins)

Wales and daughter of his old mentor Warwick. They retired to Middleham Castle and had one son, Edward, who was born around 1473. Increasingly absorbed in his role as Lieutenant of the North, Richard also took part in the French campaign of 1475, where peace was negotiated without bloodshed. He remained loyal to Edward throughout as his motto, 'loyaulte me lie', dictated, and proved himself to be a pious and diligent lord. Together, the brothers exhumed their father's body from his tomb at Pontefract and laid York to rest in an elaborate ceremony at the Church of St Mary and All Saints at Fotheringhay in 1476.

Yet cracks would soon appear in this show of unity. George, Duke of Clarence, had previously opposed Edward in the hope of ruling England himself one day but Edward had chosen to reconcile with his brother. When Isabel, Duchess of Clarence, died in 1476, probably as the result of a complication arising from childbirth, George blamed the queen for bewitching his family. His behaviour grew increasingly erratic and aggressive, until he burst into a session of Parliament, making threats and curses against the king. After years of having been forgiven for his disloyalty, this effectively signed his death warrant. Legend has it that he was drowned in a butt, or barrel, of Malmsey wine at his own request, rather than face the executioner's axe. After 1478, Richard was Edward's only surviving brother and most trusted ally, helping run the country in the North and leading a successful military campaign against the Scots. For Richard, Anne and their son Edward, the years at Middleham might have continued to slip by, filled with service and worship, until they died peacefully in their beds. Yet a different future was on the horizon. Everything changed in the spring of 1483.

Above left: Edward IV. Richard served his older brother loyally during his lifetime. The king's premature death in 1483 reopened old wounds about his secret marriage and unleashed suppressed tensions at his court. (Courtesy of David Baldwin)

Above right: The royal arms as displayed in the pulpit of St Mary and All Saints, Fotheringhay. The black bull of Clarence is on the left, and the white boar of Gloucester on the right. (Courtesy of Josephine Wilkinson)

Right: The Elizabethan tomb of Richard's parents, Richard, Duke of York, and Cecily Neville, at St Mary and All Saints, Fotheringhay. (Courtesy of David Baldwin)

3

Princes in the Tower: 1483

On 9 April 1483, Edward IV died. Just three weeks short of his forty-first birthday, he was still a young man and his final illness came on suddenly. Mancini stated that he caught a cold after a fishing trip on the Thames, which may have developed into pneumonia, although later hostile sources stress the king's corpulence and unhealthy appetites. He languished for a few days, while his doctors tried to diagnose the illness, before taking a turn for the worse. Edward probably had at least a few hours' warning of his death, long enough to think about the future of his family and his realm. He had made a will back in 1475, before invading France, but that had been eight years ago. Since then, the political situation had changed and he had not expected to die so soon. He humbly made his peace with God and bade farewell to his family. Ten days later, his body was laid to rest in St George's Chapel at Windsor Castle.

Back in 1475, there had been no doubt about Edward's intentions for the future. His eldest son would inherit his title, even though the prince was only four years old at that point. His first will states 'oure son Edward' was to 'succeede us in the corone of England', which would result in the 'seure and restfull governance' of the realm.[1] This wish would not have changed by 1483, when the boy had reached twelve years of age, but the question remained as to who would be in a position to influence him. With the experience of Henry VI's childhood still within living memory, it was clear that a Protector was required for the two or three years remaining of his minority, until Edward would be able to rule for himself. Whoever held this position was likely to become the real power behind the throne, although the king could choose to reject them on attaining his majority.

The candidates were the queen's Wydeville relatives, particularly her brother Anthony, who had supervised the boy's education at Ludlow, and his paternal uncle, Richard, Duke of Gloucester. It is likely that on his deathbed, King Edward anticipated some rivalry between his relatives and tried to make some additions to his previous will. These may have been written down by a scribe, or possibly were merely spoken, if time was running out. The Croyland Chronicler states that Edward added codicils on his deathbed, 'but what a sad and unhappy result befell all these wise dispositions of his'.[2]

The Yorkist court had long contained undercurrents of dissatisfaction. Edward's strong authoritarian presence had kept various factions in place during his lifetime but his death threatened to open old wounds. Londoner Robert Fabyan wrote of 'gruge and unkindness' at court over the 'rule and kepynge of the yonge kinge'.[3] In the aftermath of his death in April, a struggle for control began that was quickly to escalate. Five days later, the news reached Ludlow, where the young Prince of Wales had his household. Soon he set out on the journey to London, under the protection of Anthony Wydeville, both anticipating an imminent coronation. His mother had hoped for a larger force to accompany him south but Parliament ruled against her, unwilling to cause fear by allowing a significant body of men to march across the country.

The news reached Middleham Castle two days later. After arranging prayers to be said for his brother at York Cathedral, Richard headed for the capital, meeting with the Duke of Buckingham en route. Together they intercepted the young Edward V's train and after an initial show of friendship, ordered the arrest of Wydeville and other lords the following morning. His motives in doing this are unclear. It may be that he feared a conspiracy by the queen's family, or that as a royal duke he refused to be excluded from the Protectorship in favour of their unsuitable rule. At Stony Stratford, he took his young nephew into his care for the remainder of the journey. The news of his actions reached London late that night, causing chaos. Queen Elizabeth fled her apartments and took up residence in sanctuary with her children. The Marquess of Dorset, her son by her first marriage, proposed raising an army to recapture Edward but lacked public support. Parliament restored a temporary calm by explaining that Richard was acting to protect the interests of all involved. To aid the situation, he also sent a letter, promising an early date for the boy's coronation. At this stage, it seemed to be a simple struggle among those wishing to control the young king.

When they arrived in the capital on 4 May, Edward was accompanied to the Bishop of London's Palace but was not permitted to see his mother, who remained in sanctuary in Westminster. Soon after that, he was taken to the Tower, which was the traditional residence for kings prior to their coronation. Arrangements were made for the ceremony, robes were sewn and the nobility of England gathered to witness the start of the next York king's reign. A date of 24 June was set. Parliament proposed to meet the following day, with the intention of confirming

Left: Crosby Hall. Richard acquired this as his London home by 1483, when he used it to meet members of his council prior to his succession. In 1910, it was dismantled and removed brick by brick to its present location in Chelsea. (Courtesy of Jos)

Below: 'Richard, Duke of Gloucester respectfully greets his nephews', by H. Sidney (1884), from *Scenes from Shakespeare for the Young*, ed. C. Alias (1885). (Courtesy of David Baldwin)

The White Tower. Richard's nephews, Edward V and Richard of York, were gradually seen less and less through the summer of 1483, until they disappeared from sight permanently. They may have been withdrawn to a more secure location in the Tower, like the White Tower, where a box of bones was found by workmen in 1674. (Courtesy of Sean Murphy)

Right: Edward V. Still classed as an English king, in spite of the fact that he was never anointed, he reigned from 9 April until 25 June 1483. (Courtesy of David Baldwin)

Far right: The Princes in the Tower (1832) by J. E. Millais. (Courtesy of Jonathan Reeve JR1588b61p620 14501500)

Richard as the young king's Protector. Edward V settled into his spacious rooms to wait. He would never leave them.

What happened next still divides historians today. Two months after entering the capital with his nephew, Richard would be crowned King of England. Today, his actions appear dichotomic, allowing for very different readings of his character and motives: it all depends upon the question of when exactly he began to aim at the throne, and determining this is difficult in the least. Richard did not leave a diary, and only a few letters and state papers survive that give clues about his aims. Ultimately, historians can speculate as much as they like but only one person knew what his true feelings were. That person was Richard.

Some have interpreted Richard as pursuing his own ambitions from the start, following the lead of hostile chroniclers like Thomas More, Polydore Vergil and Raphael Holinshed. This reading presents him as having been driven by greed or ruthlessness to remove his nephews from the line of succession and replace Edward V as king: it came to its most famous fruition in Shakespeare's play and usually lays the blame for the death of the Princes in the Tower at Richard's door. This is part of a Tudor dialectic driven by political, moral and cultural forces. It imagines Richard heading to Stony Stratford with the intention of seizing the person of the king in order to displace him, either as the engineer of events or as a powerful and successful reactionary.

The revisionist school of thought, proposed by historical Ricardians such as George Buck, Horace Walpole and Josephine Tey, presents a loyal, noble figure who intended to protect his nephew and preserve the rights of the House of York. This was the case until late June when information surfaced regarding Edward V's reputed illegitimacy, prompting his uncle to take the difficult step of declaring him unable to rule. Then, as the next adult male heir, he reluctantly accepted Parliament's offer of the throne. Theories following this line may also suggest that the princes either escaped or were murdered by the Duke of Buckingham or Henry VII's mother, Lady Margaret Beaufort.

Of course the real Richard was a complex individual in an extremely volatile and pressured situation. People do not always act consistently and seeking to explain his actions in 1483 in comparison with his life before may be a misdirection. The truth of his behaviour probably lies somewhere between these extremes, both of which have been successfully explored in popular culture. Increasingly today, historians are attempting to find a middle way when it comes to understanding his actions.

Although Richard's motivation will continue to provoke debate, the actual events of summer of 1483 are easier to pinpoint. Elizabeth Wydeville and her children had remained in sanctuary at Westminster ever since the arrest of her brother Anthony and son Sir Richard Grey. Richard's attempts to negotiate with her failed and his attitude towards the ex-queen soon changed; perhaps he saw her confinement as a statement of antagonism. This is seen most clearly in the letters he sent north to his supporters in York, urging them to assist him 'against the Queen, her bloody adherents and affinity' who 'doth intend to murder and utterly destroy us ... and the royal blood of this realm'.⁴ Discussions regarding the Protectorship and coronation progressed until something triggered an unexpected act of aggression.

It is difficult, perhaps impossible to establish exactly what that something was. At a council meeting in mid-June, William, Lord Hastings, the former confidant of Edward IV, was abruptly arrested. This was odd because it was in fact Hastings who had written to Richard to break the news of Edward IV's death, and as late as 20 May, Richard had appointed him Master of the Mint. To all appearances, he was a staunch Yorkist ally, but mid-way into the meeting, Richard turned against him and summoned the guards to take him away. Hastings was denied any trial or chance to respond; he was executed almost at once. The mistress he had shared with Edward, Jane Shore, was accused of witchcraft along with Elizabeth. In this might lie a grain of the truth; if Richard genuinely believed himself to be labouring under some sort of curse, he needed to act decisively. It would be a mistake to overlook the degree to which sorcery was considered to be a real and far-reaching part of medieval life. It would also explain why five others, arrested along with Hastings, were later freed without charge, when Richard's fears had subsided. Alternatively, the episode may have been designed to remove an obstacle to Richard's plans and send a clear message to his opponents.

Three days later, Richard, Duke of York, Edward V's nine-year-old brother, was removed from his mother in sanctuary and sent to the Tower. A contemporary letter by Simon Stallworth describes him being met by Richard 'with many loving words' and that he was 'merry' at the prospect of reunion with Edward.⁵ The elder boy was signing documents as king up until 17 June, just five days before his anticipated coronation.⁶ The day came and went. On 22 June, a sermon delivered at St Paul's Cross by Dr Ralph Shaw or Shaa claimed that Edward V and his siblings were illegitimate and that 'bastard slips shall not take deep root'. It was alleged that their father had already been contracted to another woman, Eleanor Butler, *née* Talbot, before he married Elizabeth Wydeville. This meant that their

The Princes in the Tower, from a stained-glass window in Canterbury Cathedral. Edward succeeded his father on his death in April but at the age of twelve, he would have been governed by a Protector until such time as he came of age. His brother Richard, aged nine, had already been married to the heiress Anne Mowbray (who had subsequently died) at the time of their disappearance. (Amy Licence)

marriage was considered invalid, which would disinherit all the children born after it. Eleanor had died back in 1468 and no record of the union had been made. Marriages could be forged on simple verbal promises called 'handfasting', but the information given to Richard by Robert Stillington, Bishop of Bath and Wells, suggested he may have officiated at a ceremony, or known who had. This could not be proven, but it was to change the course of English history forever and seal the fate of Edward IV's sons. The following month, the boys' personal servants were dismissed from the Tower, with the last eyewitness account being made by their physician, Dr Argentine. Some reports claimed they had been moved into more private apartments but they were never seen again.

Various theories have developed in the intervening centuries about the fates of the princes. They may have both died at the hand of either Richard, the Duke of Buckingham, Margaret Beaufort or some unknown assassin. Others hope that one or both of the boys escaped and turned up later as pretenders to the throne, or else lived out lives of quiet obscurity. When Italian diplomat Mancini left England in July that year, he stated that the princes had disappeared from view but that he did not know what had happened to them. Their servants were removed on 13 July, including Dr Argentine, who reputedly spoke of the elder boy's sense of impending doom.[7] The Great Chronicle says that 'the children of King Edward were seen shooting and playing in the garden of the Tower by sundry times' during the mayoralty of Sir Edmund Shaa, perhaps related to the Dr Ralph who had declared their illegitimacy. Shaa's term in office ended in October that year. Croyland states the princes were in the Tower when Richard went on progress on 20 July; Rous implies they were dead by August and Molinet also places such an event around the same time. London-based Robert Fabyan, who died in 1513, wrote that according to common fame, Richard 'put unto secret death the two sons of his brother'. Richard's silence on this is frustrating. He never accused anyone else of the crime, nor took the opportunity to display the bodies. If he had discovered the boys' killer, or if their deaths had been caused by illness or accident, this would have cleared his name. Some would say his silence speaks volumes.

The trail might have gone cold there, if it had not been for a discovery made by some workmen during the reign of Charles II. In 1674 a box of bones was discovered buried under a stairwell in the White Tower, which appeared to contain the remains of two children. These were submitted to forensic analysis in 1933, which concluded that they may have been the bones of the princes, according to age and the approximate year of death. The two skeletons may have been contaminated by other matter, having initially been removed from the box, but as far as was ascertainable, they measured 4 feet 10 and 4 feet 6½ inches, compatible with the ages of the boys in 1483.[8] These findings were re-examined and disputed by Ricardian Paul Murray Kendall in the 1950s on account that it

The White Tower. From the late fifteenth century, this manuscript illumination shows the Tower of London much as it would have looked in Richard's time. (Courtesy of Jonathan Reeve JR992b4p640 14501550)

The staircase in the White Tower, under which workmen in 1674 uncovered a box of bones buried under rubble. The bones were examined in the 1930s and although the findings indicate they may have matched the princes' ages, there was still room for doubt regarding their genders and whether the bones had been contaminated or mixed with others. The remains are currently in an urn in Westminster Abbey and there are no plans to subject them to further tests. (Courtesy of Stephen Porter)

could not be disproved that they were female. The bones were placed in a sealed urn in Westminster Abbey and have not been opened since. No modern court of law could convict anyone for the boys' murder based on the existing evidence. In fact, the 1984 jury of BBC drama *The Trial of King Richard III* acquitted their uncle of the crime. At the present time there are no future plans to reopen the urn and conduct further testing. Perhaps the truth about the princes' fates will never be known.

In late June 1483, events moved quickly. The coronation of Edward V was postponed indefinitely and his Parliament was cancelled. On 24 June, the Duke of Buckingham addressed the assembled lords, reminding them that the role of a king was not suited to a child and stirring memories of civil discontent under the previous regime. Two days of discussion followed. During this time, Anthony Wydeville, the king's half-brother Sir John Grey, and the loyal Sir Thomas Vaughan, were executed without trial, accused of having plotted against Richard. Then, on 26 June, Richard accepted the throne, rode in state to Westminster and seated himself on the King's Bench. There he took the sovereign's oath, and that evening his rule was proclaimed at St Paul's Cathedral.

Richard's coronation took place in Westminster Abbey on 6 July. The royal seamstresses were hard pushed to complete their work on the purple cloth of gold, tassels, laces and white silk that the king and queen would wear. Richard walked barefoot in procession behind the leading magnates and churchmen of the day, while Anne followed in a circlet of gold set with precious stones, her train carried by Margaret Beaufort. Heralds announced their approach and solemn songs were

Richard being offered the crown
at Baynards Castle on 26 June
1483. Sigismund Goetze in
the Royal Exchange, London.
(Courtesy of Jonathan Reeve
JR1569b13fp718)

sung as they neared the altar. There, they were anointed by the Archbishop of
Canterbury, before changing into robes made of cloth of gold and kneeling in
prayer. Two empty thrones awaited them on a platform covered with red worsted.
The thousands of men Richard had summoned from the North remained in the
capital, being placed at strategic locations along the route. Other precautions
included the imposition of a 10 p.m. curfew for three nights and the forbidding of
Londoners to bear arms. Some might interpret this as the new regime anticipating
opposition; alternatively it may be considered a sensible precaution.

Three months after the death of Edward IV, England had a new king. But it was
not the twelve-year-old boy the country had been expecting. Instead they were to
be ruled by Richard III.

4

King: 1483–1485

For such a controversial king, still able to incite passionate debate today, Richard's reign was a short one. Twenty-six months separated his coronation and death, hardly sufficient time for him to fulfil the potential he may have possessed, but long enough to have made a mark on history. Additionally, the rumours and rebellions which began a few months after his coronation made his tenure on the throne a process of constant reaction to domestic and foreign dangers.

It all began in a blaze of glory. The post-coronation celebrations might have been planned hurriedly but they were nonetheless magnificent. Dressed in their cloth of gold, Richard and Anne processed from the Abbey into the Great Hall of Westminster Palace, where they took their places at a marble table. Around 3,000 people attended the coronation feast, but the best food, including the dressed peacock, was reserved for the new king and queen, who ate from dishes made of gold, silver and gilt. The Duke of Norfolk led the other lords in waiting on the royal pair, carving their meat and pouring their wine, with feasting lasting five hours. The whole of London was *en fête*.

Across the rest of the country though, rumours were spreading. In an age of imperfect communication, the rapid events of recent weeks left people in small, far-flung communities wondering who was in charge of the country and questioning exactly how this had come about. It was necessary for Richard to show himself to his subjects and demonstrate the strength and majesty of the new regime. Two weeks after the coronation, he set out, accompanied by a huge retinue, and travelled west through the Thames valley before heading north. Joined en route by his wife and son, the party arrived in York in late August. The city was ready to welcome him. Richard's secretary, John Kendal, had written ahead to warn them of the king's advance and the packed streets were hung with 'cloth of arras [and] tapestry work',[1] while the city dignitaries came out to meet him in scarlet gowns. On 7 September, after a week of celebrations, Richard and Anne's son was

York Minster Library was once the chapel of the Archbishop of York's palace. This was where Richard invested his son as Prince of Wales in 1483. (Courtesy of David Baldwin)

invested as Prince of Wales in a splendid ceremony at York Minster. As Croyland relates, Richard repeated his coronation and little Edward, then aged somewhere between seven and ten, was given 'the insignia of the gold wand and the wreath upon [his] head'.[2] The Grafton Chronicle said that in York, Richard was held in such honour by the common people that 'they extolled and praised him far above the stars'.[3] In his absence though, malcontents in the South were far from starry-eyed. A number of uprisings were being hatched to challenge his position.

Richard was in Lincoln when news reached him of trouble brewing in the capital. Elizabeth Wydeville had joined forces with Margaret Beaufort, whose position as the widow of Edmund Tudor, one of Henry VI's half-brothers, placed her closer to the throne. With the Lancastrian king and his son dead, Margaret's son, Henry Tudor, now emerged as a possible figurehead for opposition to Richard's reign. Elizabeth was still in sanctuary but using a doctor as a go-between, they plotted the marriage of Henry to the eldest Yorkist princess, Elizabeth of York, now technically illegitimate. The nature of this plan is not altogether clear; it depended upon what the women believed to have happened to the Princes in the Tower. If they thought that the boys were still alive, it may have been an attempt to restore

Elizabeth of York, Richard's niece, the eldest daughter of Edward IV. At some point after she came out of sanctuary in March 1484, Elizabeth went to Richard's court: she was definitely there by Christmas, when Croyland reports that rumours spread regarding Richard's intentions towards her. He made a public declaration the following spring that he was not intending to marry her. (Courtesy of Amanda Miller)

Edward V to the throne, with Tudor's help. This agrees with the theories of a French bishop, Thomas Basin, who was recording rumours that reached the Continent. If, however, they had been told that Edward V and his brother had been killed, the plan would have been focussed on Henry's attempt to remove Richard III and take the throne himself, with Elizabeth of York as his wife.

Other uprisings in the South suggested a wider sense of discontent. The Croyland Chronicler listed unrest in at least nine counties, where people began to 'murmur greatly' and became determined to 'avenge their grievances' by gathering in 'meetings and confederacies'.[4] This source, although possibly distant from London, believed that initially the uprising was in the name of the princes, 'in order to deliver them from ... captivity'.[5] Croyland also recorded that there were plans made to assist Elizabeth Wydeville's daughters in an attempt to flee sanctuary 'in disguise' and find safety abroad. In case any 'fatal mishap' did befall their brothers, they may still enable the kingdom to 'fall into the hands of the rightful heirs'.[6] At the same time, the writer noted that a rumour was spreading that the princes 'had died a violent death, but it was not sure how'. The focus of their plans now became Henry Tudor.

Then, though, Croyland reports that the Duke of Buckingham, Richard's former ally, had become involved in the revolt. Today, it is usually referred

Brecon Castle (Powys). Bishop Morton was imprisoned here in 1483, and is said to have turned the Duke of Buckingham against Richard. (Courtesy of David Baldwin)

to as his rebellion. Buckingham had been central to the events of that summer, joining with Richard on his march south, supporting his claim to the throne and petitioning Parliament to offer it to him; at the coronation, he had been awarded an 'especial gift' of 8 yards of blue cloth of gold and 8 yards of black velvet.[7] He was also a cousin to the king, with his own, weaker, claim to the throne, and had been married young to a sister of Elizabeth Wydeville. This marriage had bred considerable resentment in him, as he considered Katherine not to be a suitable wife for his status. Other recent events might have influenced him though. Since the summer, Bishop Morton, a known ally of Margaret Beaufort, had been held under house arrest at Buckingham's residence at Brecknock Castle. Morton had been arrested during the session of Parliament where Hastings had lost his head; perhaps he had been influencing the duke or imparted something to him since that time.

Richard ordered armies to be mustered and marched south. Already though, the forces of resistance were crumbling and the various sections failed to co-ordinate. Their intention had been to divert the king's attention by a mock attack on London by the Kentish men while Buckingham marched west and Tudor landed on the South Coast. A significant number may have been involved but the entirety lacked cohesion; the rebels in the South East were swiftly subdued by those loyal to Richard while others deserted. In exile in Brittany, Tudor launched his invasion force only to beaten back by storms, while Buckingham's attempts to travel south failed after the River Severn rose and became impassable. Richard had reacted swiftly and decisively. Unable to unite the forces, Buckingham soon realised he had allied himself with a lost cause.

The duke's motives for rebelling against his former friend have long been the topic of debate. While many of the rebels had been loyal supporters of Edward IV and his son, Buckingham had been instrumental in Richard's rise to power, and his actions in the early autumn of 1483 constituted a considerable betrayal. A number of possibilities have been suggested, ranging from a general sense of disaffection with the new king, to the duke's own desire for the throne, to the fact that he believed Richard had been responsible for the deaths of the princes. Tudor historian Polydore Vergil suggested that Buckingham was aggrieved that Richard denied him the grant of some significant lands but, in fact, he had just been granted the Bohun estates he coveted. Others suspect, more cynically, that the duke believed the tide was turning against Richard and seized the chance to overthrow what he believed to be a doomed regime.

It is unlikely that Buckingham rebelled alone; a number of other leading figures supported the uprisings, including Bishop Morton and Thomas Grey, son of Elizabeth Wydeville. In his literary version, Thomas More reconstructs the conversations his mentor, Morton, had with Buckingham, crediting him with placing the idea in the duke's head. However, Buckingham was the most visible and the closest to Richard. He attempted to seek sanctuary, possibly with the intention of reaching the coast and joining Tudor in Brittany, as Grey did. Some reports have him disguised as a labourer as he fled south. After Richard had publicly declared Buckingham a traitor, though, it was far more difficult for him to preserve any degree of secrecy and his location was soon betrayed. He was convicted of treason and beheaded in the marketplace at Salisbury on 2 November. For the moment, the threat had been suppressed. That Christmas, though, Henry Tudor swore an oath in Rennes Cathedral that he would invade again and take Elizabeth of York as his wife. Almost from the start of his reign, Richard was forced to confront opposition at home and abroad; the threat of Tudor's return was never to go away.

In January 1484, Richard's first and only Parliament met at Westminster. One of its first Bills was Titulus Regis, which confirmed the invalidity of the marriage between Edward IV and Elizabeth Wydeville and excluded their offspring from succession. Henry VII would later attempt to destroy all copies of this Act, which impugned the lineage of his wife and her family. However, one survived and was discovered in the seventeenth century. It defames Edward IV's reign as morally and politically corrupt and claims that Elizabeth Wydeville had snared him illegally through the use of witchcraft.[8] Other enactments of the January Parliament concerned the administration of justice, including the election of incorruptible jury men, attacks on the deceptions practised in property sales, the extension of existing bail laws and the protection of lands belonging to prisoners. A court of poor requests had also been established the previous December. Richard also turned his mind to the future, to the succession of his son, to whom the lords were obliged to swear loyalty in the event of his own death. Then he came to an agreement with Elizabeth Wydeville, who was still in sanctuary with her five daughters. He swore a public oath to protect the girls, whose ages ranged from eighteen to four, and arrange suitable marriages for them, whereupon they finally emerged.

Elizabeth's actions have been criticised by some historians and cited as evidence that she did not believe Richard responsible for the deaths of her sons. However, she was in no doubt that he had ordered the executions of her brother Anthony and her son by her first marriage, Sir John Grey. Sanctuary was only ever intended as a short-term measure and having been there for nine months, with her role in that autumn's uprising suspected, if not proven, Elizabeth was not in a strong position. Margaret Beaufort had paid for her involvement by having her lands confiscated, although these were actually placed in the hands of her husband, Sir Thomas Stanley. There was no benefit of hindsight available to Elizabeth in the spring of 1484; for all she knew, Richard's reign may continue for twenty or thirty more years. There was little real alternative to making the best of the situation. She could do nothing to help her sons by then, but she could act in the interests of her daughters. By insisting that Richard swore a public oath to protect her girls, she had done all she could to allow them some sort of future. Aware of Henry Tudor's oath, Richard may have seen this as his opportunity to marry off Edward IV's daughters, thus denying his adversary this chance.

In March, Richard set off again on progress, through the Midlands to Nottingham. Having led an invasion against the Scots at the end of his brother's reign, he now prepared to strike against them again, gathering resources for an imminent attack. While they were staying at Nottingham Castle, terrible news reached Richard and Anne from Middleham. Their only son, Edward, Prince of

Ad Dei gloriam et in piam memoriam
Collegiam fieri fecit　Anno domini

Ricardi tertii Regis Anglie qui hanc
m.cccc.lxxviii.

A memorial window depicting Richard on the lower-left light (detail top picture), his son Edward kneeling behind him, and his wife Anne is in the lower right (detail bottom picture). (Courtesy of David Baldwin)

Wales, had died after a short illness. Having spent most of his life in the North, Edward remains a shadowy figure, about whom many authors have been quick to draw conclusions of 'sickliness' and ill health. This may have been the case, but equally, he may have simply suffered one of the many maladies that contributed to the high levels of childhood mortality during this time. The cause of his death remains unknown, as does his final resting place. The impressive carved tomb, topped with a recumbent child in coronet and robes, at Sheriff Hutton is frequently assigned to him, but in fact it is empty. This is not to say it is not Edward's memorial, or that he does not lie nearby, but the exact location of his bones remains unknown.

Prince Edward's death was a tragedy for Richard and Anne on a personal level. The Croyland Chronicle described their 'sudden grief' as sending them into a state 'almost bordering on madness'. In a wider sense, it was a political disaster. Without an heir, Richard's reign was less secure, with only him standing between any challenger and the crown. He knew the news would reach Henry Tudor in Brittany, who was planning his next invasion. Briefly, Richard considered naming Clarence's son, the ten-year-old Earl of Warwick, as his successor. He also had an illegitimate son of his own, John of Pontefract or Pomfret, probably fathered before his marriage during his year-long residency of Pontefract Castle from

Anne Neville (centre), Prince Edward of Lancaster, Anne's first husband (left) and Richard III (right). (Courtesy of Jonathan Reeve JR1731b90fp109c14001500)

April 1471. Although he may not have been physically present for the entire year, his regular visits may have resulted in the conception of this son, whose name suggests his mother was a local woman. This time frame would have made John around eleven or twelve in 1484; he would be promoted to Captain of Calais the following year. Eventually though, perhaps mindful of the fate of the princes, Richard settled his succession in favour of his nephew, John de la Pole, Earl of Lincoln. The son of his sister Elizabeth, Duchess of Suffolk, John was already an adult and therefore capable of independent rule.

Richard spent that summer overseeing the now scaled-down Scottish plans and establishing a formal Council of the North, to meet every quarter sessions at York and supervise the peace while he was in the South. Its authority came from the king but the Earl of Lincoln was at its head. Then Richard returned to London where, in August, he ordered the removal of Henry VI's bones from Chertsey Abbey to St George's Chapel, Windsor. Miracles had been reported in Henry's name and a fledgling cult had developed around the memory of his pious life and violent death.

Far left: Henry VI portrayed as a saint in about 1500 on a Ludham church screen in Norfolk. Henry VII attempted to have him canonised, but was not successful. (Courtesy of Jonathan Reeve JR1561folio6)

Left: Richard Neville, Earl of Warwick, also known as 'Warwick the Kingmaker'. He was Anne Neville's father and Richard's mentor, training him in the chivalric arts at Middleham Castle. (Courtesy of David Baldwin)

Richard commissioned a new alabaster tomb, with a figure of Henry recumbent on top amid heraldic devices. This now no longer exists, having been dismantled around 1600. A slab on the floor commemorates him there today.

Next, Richard was forced to deal with a new danger. He had returned to Nottingham, to meet a Scottish delegation and arrange a match between the son of James III and his niece, Anne de la Pole, when fresh scandal reached his ears. William Collingbourne is most famous today for having penned the lampoon beginning 'the Cat, the Rat and Lovell our Dog, doe rule all England under a Hog', which cast a slur on Richard and his chief advisors, William Catesby, Richard Ratcliff and Francis, Lord Lovell. Collingbourne was a previous employee of Richard's mother, Cecily Neville, and was part of what Professor Michael Hicks refers to as continual 'haemorrhage of new defections'.[9] His fate of being hanged, drawn and quartered in December 1484 has sometimes been judged as overly harsh on Richard's part, yet Collingbourne was far more than a scurrilous poet. He had been sending letters to Henry Tudor, inviting him to land at Poole, in Dorset, whereupon the English people would rise up against their king and support his overthrow. That winter must have been a difficult one for Richard, with his son dead and his wife soon to be ailing, and knowing that Tudor's invasion would land sometime in the following year. Hindsight now informs us just how significant that event would prove.

5

Henry Tudor: 1457–1485

In Richard's eyes, the Tudor claim to the throne was a tenuous one. However, the twenty-eight-year-old Henry certainly had royal blood, from both sides of his family. He was the grandson of Henry V's French queen, Catherine of Valois, but as a result of her illicit second marriage. Catherine had borne the future Henry VI in 1521 and been widowed soon afterwards, moving to Wallingford Castle. The site now lies in ruins, but in its heyday it was a prosperous and luxurious stronghold overlooking the Thames. About six years later, the dowager queen fell in love with a Welsh squire named Owen Tudor, who was the keeper of her wardrobe; legend has it that the handsome servant fell into her lap while dancing. The Tudor family had come to London to re-establish their fortunes after Owen's grandfather was ruined after rebelling against the new Lancastrian regime back in 1400. It was to prove a spectacular return to favour.

Catherine's eldest son, the new king, Henry VI, was only six at the time when her liaison with Tudor began. Whoever controlled the boy king ruled the country, so he had been left in the care of his two uncles, John, Duke of Bedford, and Humphrey, Duke of Gloucester. As a young woman Catherine was permitted little influence over her boy, and after decades of war with France, her nationality also led to her being distrusted. Parliament feared that she may try to play a greater role if she were to remarry and gain the support of an influential husband from the English nobility. Therefore, an Act of Parliament had forbidden her to wed again until her son came of age. Lonely and in love, Catherine and Owen were wed in secret, but went on to have several children, the eldest being Edmund, who arrived in around 1430. This was probably the worst-kept secret at court, but if Parliament knew about it, they may well have turned a blind eye, judging that Tudor's lowly status rendered him less of a threat.

After his mother's death in 1438, Henry VI supervised the education of his younger half-siblings. The two elder boys, Edmund and Jasper, were prepared for a life at court, being granted the titles of Earl of Richmond and Earl of Pembroke respectively, while the younger siblings were destined for the church.[1] After a period of uncertainty, Owen was welcomed at court by the king and would remain his stepson's loyal adherent, fighting on his behalf in the Wars of the Roses. Henry also arranged an important marriage for Edmund, to his young kinswoman, the Lancastrian heiress Lady Margaret Beaufort. Her claim to the throne was stronger than Edmund's but like his, it came through an illegitimate line. The Beaufort descent derived from a liaison between a younger son of Edward III, John of Gaunt, and his mistress Katherine Swynford. Their later marriage had legitimised their children, but they had been barred from the succession. Margaret was the only child of their eldest son. She had previously been promised as a child bride to John de la Pole but, due to her age at the time, that connection was easily annulled and her wardship was granted to Edmund. Their wedding took place in 1455. He was twenty-six; she was twelve.

By the summer of 1456, Margaret had conceived. As a result of the fighting that had broken out between the houses of York and Lancaster, Edmund Tudor had been imprisoned at Carmarthen Castle, and, shortly after his release, died from an outbreak of plague that hit the town. Alone and seven months pregnant, Margaret travelled to Pembroke Castle in west Wales, the home of her brother-in-law Jasper. It was there, on 28 January 1457, in a tiny tower room, that she gave birth to Henry Tudor. Although little evidence survives of the occasion, it was likely to have been a life-threatening ordeal for the thirteen-year-old, whose immature body was unlikely to have reached sufficient height or weight to easily facilitate a child's arrival. Her confessor, John Fisher, would later describe her as never having been a 'woman of great stature'.[2] Given the statistics on infant and maternal mortality, she and her baby were lucky to survive, although she may well have suffered such significant injuries as to prevent her bearing more children.

A year later, Margaret remarried. Her new husband was Henry Stafford, Earl of Buckingham, but soon her maternal fortunes changed. After the Lancastrian forces were defeated at Towton in 1461, the wardship of the four-year-old Henry was awarded to loyal Yorkist Lord Herbert of Raglan. There the boy remained until 1469, when Herbert himself became a casualty of the continuing civil war, executed by rebels led by the Earl of Warwick. Although the initial uprising was suppressed, the Yorkist regime was toppled again in 1470, and after Edward IV fled to exile, Henry VI was released from captivity and briefly restored to the throne. Henry visited his half-uncle at court and was shown every favour, with the king reputedly recognising him as his future heir, almost as if in a vision.

Above and below: Raglan Castle, where Henry VII grew up. (Amy Licence)

However in 1471, the exiled Edward returned, and heavy fighting at the battles of Barnet and Tewkesbury left Warwick and the Prince of Wales, Henry VI's son, dead. Within hours, the last Lancastrian king was murdered in the Tower of London, probably at the command of Edward IV. Jasper Tudor was forced into exile in Brittany, taking his fourteen-year-old nephew with him. He would not set foot on English soil again until August 1485.

Henry did not give up on his Lancastrian claim. His first attempt to invade had been defeated by a combination of bad weather and disorganisation in the autumn of 1483, but his oath to defeat Richard III and marry Elizabeth of York proved him to be serious in his opposition. He returned to Brittany, which was then under separate governance from the rest of France, ruled by Duke Francis II, and gathered a core of disaffected Wydevilles and Lancastrians around him. Richard took steps to try and oust him from exile, negotiating with the duke, although Francis refused to hand Tudor over. However, when the duke fell ill, Richard was able to come to terms with the Breton minister, Pierre Landais, and a plan was forged to return Henry to England. Elizabeth Wydeville's eldest son, Sir Thomas Grey, had been his companion in exile since fleeing England after Buckingham's failed rebellion, but was then persuaded to desert Tudor after hearing that his mother and Richard had come to terms early in 1484. He was caught attempting to return to England around the same time that Bishop Morton helped expose the Yorkist plot with Landais. At the last moment, Henry fled to France, keeping Grey in Paris as surety for the French king's financial support. From there, he planned the campaign that would eventually be fought at Bosworth.

In London, Richard was beset by a new swathe of damaging rumours. Croyland reports that Queen Anne had fallen ill around the end of 1484 and increasingly withdrew from court life. The cause of Anne's death is unknown. Aged only twenty-eight, her condition was serious and her death was anticipated, although no evidence survives to suggest that she was sickly or weak before this point. She only bore one live heir, as far as we know, and this may be indicative that she was suffering from an illness such as tubercular endometriosis, which caused low fertility. However, she may equally have been afflicted by a range of other conditions that medieval medicine and modern distance are now unable to diagnose. Her childbearing record and her premature death may not have been connected in any way.

At court that Christmas, the festivities were marked by comparisons between Anne and the radiant figure of her young niece, Elizabeth of York. Citing examples of the two women wearing similar clothing, Croyland reported that the beautiful, blonde eighteen-year-old was now the target of her uncle's affections, although it was customary for relations to wear similar clothing, particularly during ceremonies and festivities. It may even have been a complimentary gesture. But Croyland had more. Further reports cited rumours that Elizabeth would become Richard's wife as soon as her ailing aunt was out of the way. Predictably, his enemies began to spread word that Anne was being poisoned and that Richard had rejected her, avoiding her bed.

The question of Richard's relationship with Elizabeth of York has proved the inspiration for many historical novelists since. So far as the facts go, there are Croyland's comments that people were scandalised by Elizabeth appearing dressed similarly to Anne and by other shameful behaviours which he does not specify. There is also a letter reputedly written by Elizabeth to John Howard, Duke of Norfolk, which surfaced in the seventeenth century, in the hands of the Ricardian George Buck. This letter has been reconstructed, literally, from a copy of a lost original and can be read in a number of ways; some believe that in it, Elizabeth is callously wishing for the speedy death of her aunt in order to marry her uncle. This was not strictly forbidden by canon law, although a dispensation would have been required. It did transgress certain cultural and moral codes though. Others suggest that Elizabeth was referring to a Portuguese marriage that Richard was planning for her, also that the phrase that she was his in 'body and soul' was a respectful convention rather than proof of a physical relationship. Queen Anne died amid an eclipse of the sun on 16 March and was buried in Westminster Cathedral. No accounts of her funeral survive beyond the general description that its honours 'befitted the interment of a queen' but it is likely that Richard followed the usual protocol that spouses did not attend. Accounts of him weeping at her funeral stem from fiction. Croyland claims that after Anne's death, his 'countenance was always drawn'.

Six days later, ambassadors left the English court, bound for Portugal. Richard did not make plans to marry Elizabeth of York; instead, he aimed for the hand of Joanna, sister of the Portuguese king, John II. Elizabeth was sent north under the keeping of the Stanley family, ending up at Sheriff Hutton while Richard tried to match her with Joanna's cousin Manuel. There is no doubt that some of his contemporaries believed the marriage might become a reality and that it would damage the king's reputation. The rehabilitation of the Wydeville family, through Elizabeth, would also significantly affect the fortunes of many at court. Two of his closest advisors, Ratcliffe and Catesby, warned him that it would provoke a rebellion in the North among those loyal to the Neville family, who had believed the rumours that Richard poisoned Anne in order to take his niece as his wife.[3] To prevent this, Richard was forced to make a public declaration to the contrary in March 1485. The news reached Henry Tudor in Brittany and might have spurred his campaign forward; the union of Richard and Elizabeth would have robbed him of the Yorkist support he had hoped to harness. Holinshed records that he took the news as 'a matter of no small moment' and it 'nipped him at the very stomach'.[4]

Through the spring and early summer Richard waited, raising funds for his campaign, trying to predict when and where Henry would land. He mustered his troops at Nottingham and purchased guns and suits of lightweight Milanese armour. The town was ideally placed for him to repel an attack wherever it may come from; he also sent Sir Francis Lovell to the South Coast to repel any landing attempt there. On 23 June, he issued a proclamation that Tudor had no right to the English throne, but was in fact illegitimate through both his family lines. Due to his 'ambitious and insatiable covertise,' the proclamation continued, Tudor 'encroaches and usurps upon him the name and title of royal estate of this Realm'.[5] A month later, his informants brought news that Henry was preparing his fleet to depart from Harfleur. Richard was not troubled by the news; on the contrary, he was keen to seize the opportunity to confront and destroy his adversary. Tudor was inexperienced, an exile with a weak claim and scant support. He had been defeated by the English weather before and should be easily dispatched, then Richard could return to the business of ruling England. However, events would not turn out the way he anticipated.

Henry VII by Holbein. Now remembered as the founder of the Tudor dynasty, Henry's birth in 1457 went relatively unnoticed. As the son of Henry VI's half-brother, exiled in Brittany at the age of fourteen, he seemed an unlikely candidate for the English throne. With Henry VI and his son dead, the events of 1483 led some Lancastrians to look to him for leadership. Ultimately though, Henry claimed the English throne by right of conquest in 1485. (Courtesy of Elizabeth Norton)

6

Bosworth: August 1485

On 1 August, Henry Tudor set sail from Harfleur, in Normandy. Various descriptions paint him as tall, slender and habitually dressed in black, with his hair worn fashionably long and a cast in one of his blue eyes. One probable eyewitness states he had a little red mole above his chin, otherwise his face was pale.[1] Henry was twenty-eight and his last memories of England were of the aftermath of the Yorkist victory at Tewkesbury. Then, he had fled, virtually friendless; now he was returning at the head of an army.

Henry's support came primarily from a group of Lancastrian noblemen, dissatisfied with Richard's succession or loyal to the old regime, as well as a number of French and Scottish mercenaries. Holinshed places their number at around 2,000, spread through a few small ships, ready to make a second attempt to land on English soil. This time, they were lucky with the weather. 'So prosperous a wind' carried them smoothly across the channel and round the tip of Cornwall in seven days.[2] It is possible that Henry had a spy high up in Richard's government; Grafton wrote that he had been warned to avoid Southampton, where Lord Lovell awaited him, and head instead to Milford Haven, where his mother had financed an army under Sir Reginald Bray.[3] Tudor landed at Dale, near Milford Haven, on 7 August and, according to Fabyan, dropped to his knees and kissed the English soil meekly and reverently.[4] The following morning, he headed for Hereford, where Holinshed says he was received 'joyfully' by the inhabitants.

Tudor's arrival was less of a joyful occasion for many other Englishmen; in fact, it was a surprise to many that he had actually landed and put them in a considerable dilemma about whom to support. None was less certain than Henry's own stepfather, Thomas, Lord Stanley, who had married Margaret Beaufort in 1471 after she had been widowed, and his brother William. Two poems, written in the years following Tudor's invasion, reflect the situation of the Stanley family and are likely to have been commissioned by them. *The Ballad of Lady Bessiye* presents fictional conversations between Sir Thomas and Elizabeth of York,

The site of the Battle of Bosworth Field. Stretching over a huge area, the fighting between Henry Tudor's and Richard's forces was to prove decisive on 22 August 1485. (Courtesy of Phil Grain)

contriving to facilitate Tudor's defeat of Richard. The author, probably Humphrey Brereton, who bears the letters in the poem, describes how Stanley's loyalty was overcome by his charge's complaints, even though 'we must under a cloud, for wee may never trusted bee'.[5] In the poem, Richard promises to divide half his kingdom with Sir Thomas, yet Stanley chooses to support the claim and marriage of Elizabeth, reputed to have been prophesied by her father, Edward IV.

The other contemporary poem, *The Ballad of Bosworth Field*, likely to have been written by a participant or eyewitness in the Stanley's retinue, describes events leading up to and during the fighting. It outlines how Lord Stanley was summoned to attend Richard but fell ill along the way, also the advice given to the king by his advisers to crush the family. In fact, in 1485, Sir Thomas did not obey Richard's initial summons, sending his son Lord Strange instead. Suspicious of his loyalty, Richard took Strange hostage, threatening his life if his father were to defect. On the field of battle, Henry's stepfather hung back, watching the action from a hilltop; the poem recounts the action and lists those who turned out to support the invading army, like a roll call of honour, composed for those who helped win the day.

Tudor was also hoping for the assistance of Sir Walter Herbert, Earl of Pembroke, son of his former guardian. However, in 1484, Herbert had been married to Richard's illegitimate daughter Katherine Plantagenet and had received a substantial income as a result. When Henry landed in Wales, Herbert remained loyal to his new father-in-law and the positioning of his troops put Tudor to some inconvenience. Holinshed describes rumours reaching the invading army of Herbert's 'great crew' of men awaiting them at Carmarthen, which filled them with 'fearful doubt' and 'sore troubled' them and made them test their weapons.[6] It may have been messengers from Herbert who brought news to Richard of Henry's landing; some accounts have Richard Williams, Constable of Pembroke, riding 200 miles to inform Richard. This tallies with the date of 11 August, when Richard appears to have learned of the news and began to mobilise his army.

Richard should have been confident of achieving victory against the invader. He had the military experience, the pick of the country's resources and he was its anointed king; yet, according to Croyland, he anticipated that his Achilles' heel may prove to be the loyalty of some of his magnates. Before the battle, he sent out letters ordering every man of property to attend him, under pain of death and the loss of lands. On 20 August, Richard met his allies in Leicester, with their combined forces now totalling around 8,000.[7] French chronicler Molinet states that he had 60,000 combatants,[8] and even though precise numbers were hard to discern, this seems an overly generous estimation. A later Parliament roll described their 'banners spred, myghtly armed and defenced with all manner Arms, as Gunnes, Bows, Arrows, Axes and all manner articles apt and needful to get and cause mightie bataille'.[9] Richard also had the larger number of cannon, with Molinet estimating them to be 'a great number'. On 19 August, he left Nottingham for Leicester. On the same day, Tudor met with his stepfather, Sir Thomas Stanley.

Leicester had been important since Roman times, with the Normans building a castle, around which it developed into a medieval market town with an abbey and three friaries, as well as a number of active guilds. The city had Lancastrian connections earlier in the century; Henry IV had passed through it on his way to claim the throne and the young Henry VI had been given the order of the knighthood while staying in the castle. However, during the Wars of the Roses, the citizens had rallied to Edward IV's Yorkist cause, fighting with him at Towton and welcoming him when he visited. In Richard's short reign, he had already paid two visits there, staying in the castle, from where he had mustered loyal troops to defeat Buckingham in 1483. Vergil relates that on that August day, he marched into the city at dusk, as the sun was setting over the town's spires and rooftops.

The University of Leicester has been able to accurately reconstruct Richard's arrival in the city, on 20 August 1485. Approaching from Nottingham Castle, he would have entered the city through the North Gate, passing down the old High Street, busy with shops and houses, past St John's Hospital and All Saint's church. This is now Highcross Street. The modern town centre has moved away from this area but at the time of the king's arrival, the church, which still stands, would have been at the heart of the city. Seventy years before, it had witnessed the trial of Margery Kemp, a visionary and pilgrim who wrote of her experiences in one of the first ever autobiographies. Richard would recognise its Perpendicular windows and three-part tower, although he would find it quiet, as it is no longer used for worship today. St John's Hospital had a connection with the Yorkist court; since 1479, it had been in the ownership of the Newarke or 'New Work', a college of priests, through the efforts of Lord Hastings. Later it would become an almshouse for poor widows.[10]

Richard slept that night at the Blue Boar Inn on the High Street. According to legend, he brought his own bed with him. This was fairly common; as the lives of kings and their nobility were so peripatetic, large items of furniture were made to be easy to dismantle and reassemble. However, the bed that survives in a nearby manor house, reputed to be his, is too late in date. There is also a romantic tale that around a century after Bosworth, a hoard of gold coins was discovered in the bed's false bottom. Richard's chamber was decorated with a carved vine, painted in vermilion pink, which was reputedly still present into the nineteenth century. When Richard stayed there, the inn was a large, new building, catering to wealthy travellers, which survived until it was dismantled in 1836. Leicester's Travelodge now stands on the site. The following morning, he rode east out of the city, through the West Gate, over West Bridge and past the Augustinian Friary. Legend has it that he struck his spur on Bow Bridge as he left, an ill omen that had been predicted by a soothsayer or fortune teller.

The king spent the next night in less comfort, under canvas near the battlefield at Sutton Cheney. According to Shakespeare's play, Richard suffered from nightmares before the conflict, full of accusations made by the vengeful ghosts of a procession of his victims. Various dead friends and enemies, including Henry VI and his son Edward, Hastings, the Princes in the Tower and Queen Anne all come to urge Richard to 'despair and die'. This was a fairly standard literary device for writers keen to draw moral lessons from the bad deeds of pantomimic villains; other conscience-provoking apparitions appear in *Macbeth*, *Hamlet* and *Julius Caesar*. During the night, as sixteenth-century writer Hall relates, a paper was pinned to the outside of Norfolk's tent, warning him about the coming battle: 'Jacke of Norffolke be not too bold, For Dikon thy maister is bought and sold.'[11]

Whether or not this is true, it did not prevent Norfolk or Richard from taking the field in the morning.

No contemporary record survives of how Richard actually slept that night, although given his piety it is likely that he spent a portion of it in prayer. The Croyland Chronicle, written after his defeat, claims that his face was more 'livid and ghastly than usual' and that he missed breakfast and did not take Mass. This seems unlikely considering Richard's piety, although a later report cited the claim of one eyewitness, Sir Ralph Bigot, that the royal chaplains were not ready.[12] Perhaps this suggests Richard was taken by surprise. He would have been aware of Henry Tudor's presence at Atherstone, as well as the fires of his other encampments, only 3 miles off. Having arrived with around 2,000 men, the invasion army had grown on the march north, but it was still nowhere near the size of the king's troops. As a result, Tudor's captains tried to rely upon strategy rather than might, deciding to focus their attack on the vanguard of Richard's army, the first part to enter the fray.[13] Vergil describes the secret meeting between Tudor and the Stanley brothers the night before, where they took each other by the hand, amid 'mutuall salutation' and their 'myndes wer movyd to great joy'. He also reports that some of Richard's army deserted, going over to Henry's side, 'and greatly replenyshed him with good hope'. Writing between 1503 and 1513, he drew on eyewitness accounts but it must be remembered that he was working at Henry's request.

If he was troubled by deserters or bad dreams, Richard's mood on the morning of 22 August did not betray it. He assembled his men near Fenn Lane, between the villages of Dadlington, Sutton Cheney and Shenton. Vergil confirms the presence of this marsh and it was here that a recent excavation unearthed one of Richard's gilt boar badges. For centuries Ambion Hill had been the favoured location but excavations in 2010 showed that it was likely to have been fought over a mile and a half away and spread over a considerable distance.[14] They may have been between 8,000 and 10,000 strong, although some sources place the number much higher, and were led by Thomas Howard, Duke of Norfolk; his son Thomas, Earl of Surrey; and Henry Percy, Earl of Northumberland. The Tudor army was about half their size, under the command of John de Vere, Earl of Oxford, and the Breton Philibert de Chandée. Vergil estimated their number at 5,000.

The moment was approaching. Richard paraded before his assembled troops, delivering a rousing speech against the Welsh 'milksop' and displaying both the crown and a large cross. This was designed to demonstrate that God was on his side, as a pious, anointed King of England. When Tudor's army advanced mid-morning, they found themselves under bombardment from Richard's artillery. This

A battle image from Christine de Pisan. (Courtesy of the Library of Congress)

was unexpected and forced them to respond quickly, regrouping themselves around the marsh. Croyland says that at this point, Richard saw the chance to attack them; his army 'assaulted' them with arrows, making 'great showtes' before descending into brutal hand-to-hand fighting. Something made them stop and regroup though, after which Tudor's French forces appeared on Norfolk's flank with the sun behind them. They crashed through the army with longspears and probably inspired the king's comment, mentioned in a letter quoted by Alfred Spont in 1897, that 'these French traitors are today the cause of our realm's ruin'.[15] Vergil states that this was the point when Richard was urged to flee the battlefield, but he chose to remain.

Perhaps this was when he spotted Henry, coming up with the rearguard of his army. His standards of the Red Dragon, St George and the Dun Cow were visible beyond the fighting, isolated from the main body of troops. Only a small group of troops huddled about him and Oxford was too far to come to his assistance. It presented an ideal opportunity; if Richard could charge down the hill and kill his opponent, the battle was his. Although writers like Holinshed presented Richard launching himself lion-like into hand-to-hand fighting with Henry,[16] the fragment of a letter written by a surviving French soldier suggests that they were separated by a formation of pikemen. It seems likely that the hired mercenaries clustered protectively around Tudor but that he was still in grave danger, as Richard was close enough to kill his standard bearer, Sir William Brandon, and unseat Sir John Cheyney from his horse. It was at this moment, when Henry's life

Statue of Richard III in a Leicester park. (Courtesy of James Nicholls)

was in 'immediate danger',[17] that the Stanleys entered the field, on behalf of Sir Thomas's stepson. Charging downhill at the head of 3,000 men, the new arrival took Richard by surprise and he was pushed back into the nearby marshland, according to a number of writers. Here, he lost his horse and possibly his helmet before, in Molinet's words, a Welshman 'struck him dead with a halberd'.[18] A proclamation later issued by Tudor stated that he died at a place known as Sandeford, although the exact location of this has now been lost.[19]

Even historians negative in their portrayals of Richard have acknowledged his bravery on the field of battle. During his lifetime, Mancini acknowledged his 'renown in warfare', Whitelaw recognised his 'greatest valour' and Edward IV wrote of his brother's 'proved skill in military matters' in a letter to the Pope. Vergil wrote in 1520 that Richard's courage was 'high and fierce' and that he fought 'manfully'. In *The Ballad of Bosworth Field*, Richard is offered a fresh horse as a means of escaping the scene, with his knight suggesting that 'another day thou may thy worshipp win' and return again to rule. Richard replied that he would never flee so long as breath remained in his body. Then the poet, who possibly fought for the Stanleys and was in the thick of battle at this point, records that the king's crown of gold was 'hewn' from him; other sources suggest that his helmet was beaten into his head. Death would follow swiftly afterwards, but his final moments would not be fully understood until the examination of his bones in 2012. With the loss of Richard III, the battle was over.

7

Aftermath: 1485–2012

Word flew across the battlefield that the king had been killed. The fighting would have spread well away from the spot where Richard fell but gradually, the men were stilled by the news. They lowered their swords and axes and withdrew, to get their wounds attended to, to pray and to rest. According to William Hutton, writing in 1788, Richard's crown was lost in his 'last fiery struggle', being found or concealed by 'a private soldier' in a hawthorn bush, 'perhaps with a view to secure it for himself'.[1] This must have been a lightweight coronet, specifically designed to sit around his crown; Ashdown-Hill speculates that it may have been gold or gilded metal, set with jewels or paste, of sufficient value to attract a thief. It was discovered by Sir Reginald Bray and handed to Stanley, who used it to crown Henry VII at once where they stood. The Tudor dynasty had begun.

In the immediate aftermath, the field was scattered with bodies and debris. Estimates for the number of dead vary from the 10,000 given by the Castilian Report to Molinet's 300 on either side.[2] In the lull between Richard's death and the cessation of all conflict, looters moved quickly among the bodies, stripping them of clothing, valuables or pieces of armour that could be melted down. Hutton includes examples of the way local people were still using their finds from the area 300 years later: a blacksmith living nearby was still using a sword blade as a drill and an old woman used another for a spit for roasting meat.[3] Other trophies were collected too; Sir William Stanley selected a set of tapestries from Richard's baggage train while Margaret Beaufort received his personal prayer book.[4] The debris must have spread for miles and search parties would have been sent out to identify those who had been lost. Among them, in the swampy marshland, they found the body of the dead king.

As Croyland describes, Richard's body was offered 'many other insults' and treated with 'insufficient humanity'. Naked, he was thrown across the back of a horse, with a rope about his neck[5] and his hands tied. Then he was brought back into Leicester on the same route by which he had ridden out in glorious splendour.

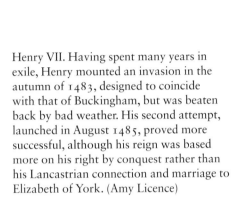

Henry VII. Having spent many years in exile, Henry mounted an invasion in the autumn of 1483, designed to coincide with that of Buckingham, but was beaten back by bad weather. His second attempt, launched in August 1485, proved more successful, although his reign was based more on his right by conquest rather than his Lancastrian connection and marriage to Elizabeth of York. (Amy Licence)

The examination of his bones revealed that he had been inflicted with at least one humiliation injury, stabbed in the buttock, probably on this journey. Legend has it that his head struck upon Bow Bridge as they arrived, just as his spur had done, by ill omen, as he rode to battle. Holinshed records that he was uncovered, with 'not so much as a clout to cover his privie members' and carried 'trussed … like a hog or calfe, his head and armes hanging on the one side of the horse, and his legs on the other side, and all besprinkled with mire and blood'. His white boar badge was 'violently razed and plucked down from every sign' because those rejoicing at his death 'wished the memorie of him to be buried with his carren corpse'.

Richard's body was put on public display. Early historians speculated that this might have been at the old Guildhall in Blue Boar Lane but in 1920, Charles Billson built a convincing case for this being at the Newarke, in the Church of the Annunciation of the Blessed Virgin Mary.[6] Holinshed has the detail that Richard 'there laie like a miserable spectacle' but a spectacle was exactly what he was intended to be. For the twenty-first-century reader, this is barbaric and unpalatable, yet it was usual medieval practice following a battle or the sudden death of a significant figure. It was vital to quell any future rumours that an enemy had survived and prevent the appearance of later pretenders. Henry needed England to know that Richard was dead. The body of the Earl of Warwick had been exhibited after his death at Barnet in 1471, as had that of Henry VI,

Above: Bow Bridge. According to a local legend, Richard rode out of Leicester across Bow Bridge and struck his spur on a stone; a wise woman had reputedly predicted he would return and hit his head on the same stone. (Courtesy of Snapper)

Left: The White Boar, a modern commemorative symbol at Bosworth, bearing Richard's motto 'loyaulte me lie'. (Courtesy of Mike Cox)

murdered in the Tower soon after. No one ever attempted to claim that they had survived. On the other hand, Richard's own inability to display the bodies of his nephews was the root of many immediate problems and the foundation of centuries of speculation.

Three days later Richard was interred in the Grey Friars church, the church of the convent of the Friars Minor. Vergil, who was later rector of Church Langton in Leicestershire, described how he was buried 'without any pompe or solemn funeral at th'abbaye of monks Franciscane at Leycester', confirming John Rous's earlier account. He appears to have received minimal funerary rites, with the recent excavations confirming his hands were still tied, crossed right over left across the pelvis and that he had not been provided with shroud or coffin. There was no evidence of any grave goods or possessions. Fabyan agrees that he was 'with little reverence buried' and the space into which he was placed was too small, with the result that his head and shoulders were thrust forwards. His body was twisted and the jaw hung open.

The nature of his burial was causing disputes even then. In York in 1491, a school teacher by the name of John Burton who was 'distempered with ale' claimed that Richard was 'a hypocrite, a crouchback and was buried in a dike like a dog'. One John Payntor came to the dead king's defence, striking Burton and telling him that Richard had, in fact, been 'buried like a noble gentleman'.[7] A noble gentleman perhaps, but not yet like a king.

A decade would pass before Richard received a tomb. Until then, he probably lay under a simple stone slab, perhaps engraved with his name. In the mid-1490s, Henry VII ordered that work should begin on a fitting memorial in alabaster and coloured marble, with £50 being paid to Walter Hilton and a further £10 1s to a James Keymer for working on 'King Rich. Tombe'. Holinshed, writing after the church and tomb had been dismantled, recorded that it had borne a 'picture' of Richard, suggestive of a flat image rather than a three-dimensional effigy.[8] Upon it was carved a Latin epitaph of sixteen lines, transcribed before 1534 by the herald Thomas Wriothesley, whose crossings out and revisions suggest he was deciphering something difficult to read. The dating of the rather convoluted final sestet suggests a composition date of 1494. Now only a 1557 copy remains of his translation. Wriothesley's earlier version has exactly the didactic and condemnatory tone that we would expect for the times:

> I here, whom the earth encloses under various coloured marble
> Was by many called Richard III.
> As Protector of the Country, on behalf of a nephew's inherited right
> I held the British Kingdoms by broken faith.
> For just sixty days less two
> And two summers, I wielded sceptres that were not mine.
> Fighting bravely in war, deservedly deserted by the English,
> I succumbed to you, King Henry VII.
> But you yourself, piously at your expense, thus honour my bones
> And cause a non-King to be revered with the honour of a King

When in twice five years less four

Three hundred five-year periods of our salvation have passed

And eleven days before the Kalends of September

I surrendered to the red rose the right it was owed.

Whoever you are, pray for my offences

That my punishment may be lessened by your prayers.[9]

However, a second version of the epitaph surfaced in the seventeenth century that made a number of alterations, including the suggestion that Richard was not the legitimate monarch. Its author was George Buck, the antiquarian who rediscovered the lost Act Titulus Regis and translated the letter reputed to be from Elizabeth of York to John Howard, Duke of Norfolk. Buck had an acknowledged Ricardian agenda, as was the case with the evidence he reinterpreted regarding Elizabeth's relationship with Richard, and admitted amending the epitaph's 'faults and corruptions'. He replaces the description 'non-king' with 'former king' and has the red rose receiving its dues, rather than them being involuntarily yielded.[10] However, he does misdate the Battle of Bosworth to 21 August. His version does not deny the earlier assertion that Richard usurped the throne but emphasises the betrayal of his men and is a slightly gentler, more sympathetic translation, and a smoother read for having been rendered into iambic pentameter:

I who am laid beneath this marble stone

Richard III, Possess'd the British Throne

My Country's Guardian in my nephew's claim

By Trust betray'd I to the Kingdom came

Two Years and Sixty Days, save two, I Reign'd

And bravely strove in Fight; but, unsustain'd

My English left me in the luckless Field

Where I to Henry's Arms was forc'd to yield.

Yet at his Cost my Corse this tomb obtains

Who piously interr'd me and ordains

That Regal Honours wait a King's Remains.

Th'Year thirteen hundred was and eighty four

The twenty-first of August, when its Pow'r

And all its Rights I did to the red Rose restore.

Reader, whoe'er thou art, thy Pray'rs bestow

T'attone my Crimes, and ease my Pains below.[11]

Right: Margaret, Richard's elder sister. Married to Charles the Bold of Burgundy in 1468, she would later support Yorkist pretenders to the throne after the advent of the Tudors. (Courtesy of Jonathan Reeve JR1565b13p704 14501500)

Far right: This plaque, at Bow Bridge, suggests that Richard's body was thrown into the river. The plaque was erected by builder Benjamin Broadbent in 1856. (Courtesy of David Baldwin)

Wriothesley recorded the epitaph just in time. Four years after his death, the Grey Friars church and its associated monastery were closed at the instigation of Henry VIII. In fact, on 10 November 1538, the keys were handed over to Henry's representative Thomas Katelyn by the priors of the Austin Friars, the White Friars, and William Gyllys, warden of Grey Friars.[12] Richard's niece, Margaret, Countess of Salisbury, was interrogated for treason a few days later and confessed that she grieved the fall of 'the houses where her ancestors lay'. The Grey Friars buildings were dismantled and sold for the roof lead and timber.[13] Ironically, some of this went to repair the nearby St Martin's church, which is now Leicester Cathedral.[14] When John Leland passed through the town in 1540, he made no mention of having seen the buildings or tomb, but referred to them in the past tense.

At the time it seemed that Richard's bones had been lost. According to John Speed in 1611, the king's remains were thrown into the River Soar and what remained of the burial site was overgrown and covered with weeds. A number of significant tombs were broken up during these years, with the treasures stripped away and the stone recycled. The bones were sometimes burned or destroyed, or they simply vanished, so Speed's theory lay within the bounds of the possible, although it remained only a theory. In addition, there was a legend that a stone drinking trough standing outside the White Horse Inn in Leicester was Richard's coffin. The diarist John Evelyn referred to it in 1654 and Celia Fiennes saw it in 1698 but the trough was broken up in the reign of George I and the slabs used to form the steps to a cellar.

To return to the site of Grey Friars church, the buildings had been flattened by 1600, when the Mayor of Leicester, Robert Herrick, built a house and laid out a garden there. He was aware of the location's history, though. The architect Christopher Wren's father visited the house in 1612 and Herrick showed him the memorial in the garden, which he recorded in his diary as being a handsome stone pillar, 3 feet high. It bore the inscription, 'Here lies the body of Richard III, some time King of England.' A century later, the land was sold on again by Herrick's descendants and a new street pattern was laid out. After that, the location remained in private hands until it was bought by Leicestershire County Council in 1914 and tarmacked over to form car parking around the time of the Second World War. It remained that way, regularly in use by the Department of Social Services until August 2012, when the diggers moved in.

Richard may well have lain undiscovered for 527 years, but in the meantime, his reputation had developed a life of its own. From the moment of his death through to the present day, he has undergone a powerful and constantly evolving afterlife, by which he has been re-interpreted, adapted and manipulated in historical accounts, chronicles, plays, poems, film, TV, portraits and novels. None of these can actually change the facts as they occurred, but in their different manifestations they tell us more about their architects than about Richard himself. Nor are they to be dismissed out of hand as simply 'biased' or 'lying'; the study of the representation of the king, the construction of a cultural caricature, almost a hyper-reality of Richard, is just as much a part of history as he was.

None of the familiar portraits of Richard were painted during his lifetime. The most iconic are also heavy in Tudor symbolism, and these can be found today in the National Portrait Gallery and Society of Antiquaries of London. In what is considered to be the earliest surviving image of Richard, painted around 1510, the king sits in an arched frame, in golden robes and chain of office. There is no sign of any deformity in his body or any particular strain to his face; given the time of composition it may even have been executed by an eyewitness. A second portrait, thought to date from around 1520, depicts him with a sensitive face, careworn perhaps, fiddling with a ring on the little finger of his right hand. In a perfect illustration of how Richard can divide interpretation, some have seen this as indicative of his cruelty while others consider it to be a comment about his humanity. Another version of this exists, which appears to be a cruder copy or version of another original work that has now been lost. Even more obvious in its symbolic purpose is the broken sword portrait, held in the Society of Antiquaries. Painted around 1550, the broken blade represents Richard's broken kingship,

Richard III. An early seventeenth-century copy of an original likeness. (Courtesy of Ripon Cathedral)

while his left shoulder has been significantly raised by a later artist. X-rays show that these additions had been made to the sitter's normal shoulders in the years following the work's completion, also that his lips and eyes were narrowed. Around twenty portraits survive, fairly formulaic in that they were copied cheaply and quickly to meet demand, but the original work from which they stemmed has been lost or destroyed.

At the same time as his portraits were being doctored, Richard's literary afterlife was developing. In 1506, Henry VII commissioned Italian scholar Polydore Vergil to write a history of England, *Anglia Historia*, although it was not published until 1534. His account includes little material favourable to Richard, immediately identifying his 'ardent desire' to be king, which he could not 'cary under any colour of honestie', so used 'spytefull practise by subtyltie and sleight' to the 'extreme detryment of the commonwelth and th'utter subvertion of his howse'. It is also the first to implicate him in the death of Edward of Westminster and the murder of the princes is presented as a fact to which a confession was made by James Tyrrell in 1502. Vergil had access to official documents and records and it has been reported that he destroyed anything that did not agree with his version of events.[15] If this is the case, we cannot even begin to speculate about what might have been lost.

Thomas More began his account of Richard's life in 1512 but did not complete it, ceasing work on it around seven years later. More was born in 1480 and served as a youth in the household of Archbishop Morton, the close associate of Margaret Beaufort, and later Henry VII. The seventeenth-century George Buck put forward the idea that Morton was the author of an original version, which More recorded and adapted, or was in the process of copying out. Internal evidence implies that some sections were written up from notes Morton made during Richard's lifetime, such as the execution of Hastings.[16] More's narrative is colourful, including fictional techniques such as imagined descriptions and conversations to achieve his didactic purposes. His 'history' is not history as we would recognise it, but it is informed by classical authors and helped 'lay the foundations for modern historiography' by rejecting the linear portrayal of events in favour of an 'admonitory narrative of people acting out their lives under the eyes of God'. More's account must be seen within the context of late medieval literary tradition, with its emphasis on hagiography, miracle and morality plays and abstract virtues and vices.

More's work was also a reflection of evolving political models. He cast Richard as an ambitious villain, plotting to usurp the throne even before the death of Edward IV. This scheming, one-dimensional version may have been accomplished by More mapping Richard's story over the literary model of the Machiavel. In fact, Niccolò Machiavelli's manuscript of *The Prince* was being circulated among his correspondents and humanist friends well in advance of its 1532 publication. One of its chapters deals with 'conquests by criminal virtue' in which a prince secures his power through cruel deeds and the execution of his political rivals. Machiavelli's advice was that all such acts should be carefully planned then executed in one swift blow, to allow his subjects the opportunity to forget them. More's motives for writing were to instruct and inspire; his work has been referred to as the first historical novel ever written[17] although it does corroborate many known facts and suggests an intimate knowledge of the events of the 1480s. Ultimately, like Vergil's, it was the account that the Tudor kings wanted it to be.

Another account was written by Edward Hall, son of a merchant grocer, born in 1497. When he was a young man, his father took on a new apprentice, the son of London chronicler Robert Fabyan, who may have been a source of Hall's interest in the period, or given him access to his father's London diaries, which had been published shortly before. It was not until 1542, though, that the first edition of Hall's chronicle *The Union of the two Noble and Illustre Families of Lancaster and York* appeared, towards the end of the reign of Henry VIII. Further editions were issued by Richard Grafton in 1548 and 1550, which included a continuum by Grafton, from the author's unfinished notes. Drawing from Vergil and More, it followed the tradition of the time in presenting the birth of the Tudor dynasty in a favourable light. Hall begins to outline the 'tragical doynges' of Richard III by saying he 'abhors' to write about 'this miserable' prince 'which by fraude entered, tyrannye proceded and by sodayn death ended his infortunate life'. The myth of the pantomime villain was well underway.

Raphael Holinshed drew on these existing accounts to produce his chronicle of English history, first published in 1577, with a revised edition 1587. This was a momentous collaboration between a number of men, begun in 1548 and incorporating much of John Leland's detailed maps of sixteenth-century England. It proved to be a popular influence on the Elizabethan playwrights, whose works retold or referenced events and individuals from the recent and distant past. One of the first of these to produce a play about Richard was Thomas Legge, the Master of Caius College, Cambridge, who also drew heavily on More. His Latin *Richard Tertius*, first performed by students of his college in 1579, presented the king not as the hunchbacked monster of Shakespeare's play but as an intelligent man driven by ambition to manipulate those around him in the Machiavellian model.

One more play was composed before Shakespeare's. The anonymous *The True Tragedy of Richard III*, written between 1585 and 1590, may have been timed to mark the centenary of the Tudor victory at Bosworth. It is a separate play from Shakespeare's proto-*Richard III*, which he named *The True Tragedy of Richard, Duke of York*, an early version of *Henry VI, Part III*. However, it may have been the play listed in 1593/4 under the alternative title *Buckingham*. This anonymous work was first recorded in performance in 1594, and appears to have been a revenge tragedy that drew on the chronicles of Hall and Hardyng. At the same time, Shakespeare was working on his own version, first recorded in 1597. His deformed villain, the fascinating and complex anti-hero whose appearance is justified as an external manifestation of inner corruption, needs little introduction. It is this version of Richard, a dramatic caricature, which has become the best-known cultural construct of the king.

Inevitably, the Bard's Richard resurfaced in later poems and plays, such as the 1614 *The Ghost of Richard III*, and the Dutch Lambert van den Bos's 1651 *Roode en Witte Roos*. In fact, the seventeenth and eighteenth centuries saw a considerable surge of interest in Richard, with Shakespeare's play being performed at the court of Charles I in 1633, to celebrate the birthday of his queen, Henrietta Maria. By the end of the century, it was being regularly enacted, under the direction of the poet laureate Colley Cibber, who adapted the play in 1699

An 1884 poster for a performance
of Richard III starring actor Thomas
Keene. The revised play, by Colley
Cibber, dominated the stage for a
century and a half, until Shakespeare's
original version was restored during
the Victorian period and has remained
the key text ever since. (Courtesy of the
Library of Congress)

for his own purposes and starred in it for almost forty years. Cibber's version cut
out several of Shakespeare's scenes and replaced them with his own speeches; he
also imported sections from other of the Bard's plays. Incredibly, this remained
the stage version for 150 years, with the lead role taken by David Garrick in
the 1740s. He was painted in the role by Hogarth, reclining in his tent on the
eve of battle. Cibber's revision was in line with an increasing Ricardian defence,
developed from the writings of George Buck by figures such as Prime Minister
Horace Walpole and even espoused by a young Jane Austen. It would not be until
1845 that Shakespeare's original version of the play was restored and performed
again.

Fictional portrayals of Richard continued though the Victorian period, with
Sir Henry Irving taking the lead role in the 1890s; a crackly recording of him
delivering the opening speech survives from 1898. Richard was also a surprising
subject of early cinema, portrayed first in 1908, then in three other silent films.
In 1996, one of these films was rediscovered after being lost for many years,
thought to be the earliest American feature film at almost an hour long, starring
Frederick Warde in the title role. The most famous screen versions since have

Richard Mansfield in the title role of Shakespeare's *Richard III*. (Courtesy of the Library of Congress)

been by Sir Laurence Olivier in 1955 and Sir Ian McKellen, in a pseudo-Fascist parallel world, in 1995. A flurry of Richard-related material surfaced again in the 1980s, with the most significant being the 1984 BBC 2 televised trial, at which leading historians gave their opinions regarding the disappearance of the princes. All the evidence was judged to be circumstantial and the jury returned a verdict of not guilty.

A brief tally of the most famous portrayals of Richard in popular culture reveals that he was a main character in at least thirty films or TV series since 1950; then there are the dozens of novels that depict his life, ranging from Josephine Tey's *A Daughter of Time* and Anne Easter Smith's *A Rose for the Crown* through to Sharon Kay Penman's *The Sunne in Splendour* and Philippa Gregory's *The Kingmaker's Daughter*, adapted by STARZ and the BBC in 2013 for the *White Queen* mini-series. He has been portrayed in fantasy novels, comics and in the popular TV historical comedy *Blackadder*, where Peter Cook, in the role, is accidentally killed at Bosworth by the hapless Rowan Atkinson. There are also counterfactual explorations of what may have happened if Richard had lived and

Richard III Road. The king has infiltrated national conciousness to the degree that his name and image frequently appear in the media and in everyday life. (Courtesy of David Baldwin)

fantasy accounts of parallel worlds where characters based on him feature, such as George R. R. Martin's *Game of Thrones*. He has been portrayed in the children's series *Horrible Histories*, made into a cartoon voiced by Sir Antony Sher, and inspired a song by the band Supergrass. Recently, he has even made his debut in vampire fiction. This does not begin to include the hundreds of non-fiction books that have attempted to rehabilitate Richard's reputation or confirm his villainy. An Amazon search reveals over 8,000 related non-fiction works, clustered round core texts by perhaps twenty established authors. Some have even attempted to carve out a more realistic middle road. No doubt more will follow.

Investigation: 2011–2013

Given the rumours about Richard's bones being thrown into the River Soar, it may seem surprising that an investigation was launched to discover his bones at all. Yet some historians were not convinced by the myth, preferring to give credence to the descriptions of the memorial in Herrick's garden and believing in the possibility that the grave had survived. It is fortunate for history that they did. The world now knows the fate of Richard's bones, which were excavated from a car park in the city of Leicester in September 2012. In a paper published in *Antiquity*, the leading archaeologists wrote that the dig arose from a desire by the Richard III Society to provide the king's 'story with a more credible conclusion than Speed's fanciful seventeenth-century tale', that the bones were dug up and disposed of. To this effect, investigations began to establish a possible site for the Grey Friars church. As it turned out, someone had already got there before them.

In 1986, historian David Baldwin wrote a paper titled *King Richard's Grave in Leicester*, outlining the possible sites for the burial. He rejected the idea that the stone drinking trough had ever held the king's bones but suggested instead that they still lay under the northern end of Grey Friars Street, where he placed the long-lost church. Placing old maps over the new street layouts, he was able to identify an area within which the Grey Friars probably lay, but was unable to be more specific. He concluded his paper with the hope that 'it is possible (though perhaps now unlikely) that at some time in the twenty-first century an excavator may yet reveal the slight remains of this famous monarch'.[1]

It was not until twenty-five years later that another historian, Annette Carson, proposed that the grave might lie under the social services car park. Then, Dr John Ashdown-Hill's *The Last Days of Richard III* linked this idea with the possibility of tracing the line of Yorkist descent and retrieving samples of DNA through the mitochondrial line. This required an unbroken line of women, passing the gene from mother to daughter from the fifteenth century to the twenty-first. It sounded almost impossible to uncover, if such a line had survived. All three of his sisters,

Anne, Elizabeth and Margaret, had married and by tracing the lineage of Anne of York, Richard's eldest sibling, Ashdown-Hill located a single surviving female, a Joy Ibsen of Canada. However, Joy passed away before the dig began, marking an end to over 500 years of mother-to-daughter DNA. This was not the end of the story though. Joy had a son, Michael, a cabinet maker who was then living in London. As a male, he could provide a sample to match with the skeleton but he was unable to transmit the gene. The line had been discovered just in time; a few more years and it would have been extinct. Ashdown-Hill was fortunate to discover a second line of descent, also able to provide DNA samples, but these relatives wished to remain anonymous.

The baton was taken up by Edinburgh screenwriter Philippa Langley, who overcame the concerns of Leicester City Council and mountains of red tape in order to commission the university to carry out an investigation. A previous dig in 2007 had uncovered no trace of the Grey Friars and Langley suspected the archaeologists had been looking in the wrong location. Having observed the proposed site back in 2004, she noticed a second, smaller car park, where, incredibly, the tarmac was marked with an 'R'. According to her account in the book she wrote about the process with historian Michael Jones, she experienced the 'strongest sensation' that she was walking on the dead king's bones. Langley launched her project in 2009 but it would prove a long process; three years would pass before everything was in place for the search to begin. In March 2011, she approached ULAS, the University of Leicester Archaeological Services, to survey the car park, and ground-penetrating radar surveys were carried out. This revealed the location of the modern utilities, such as gas and water mains, plus a series of additional unexplained anomalies. Digging was scheduled to go ahead in March 2012. Then, at the last moment, Langley's funding was pulled and the start date postponed. Langley turned to Ricardians around the world in a desperate appeal to prevent the dig from being cancelled. In the space of two weeks, she raised £13,000.

On 25 August 2012, the excavations began. There were five objectives: locating the Franciscan Friary, which was considered a likely outcome; orientating the Friary, locating the church and then the choir, and finally finding the resting place of Richard III. It was considered to be very doubtful whether this last aim would be met. The first trench was dug, running for 30 metres in a north–south direction. One of the first things to be found was a pair of leg bones, 5 metres from the north end, roughly where the letter 'R' had been painted on the tarmac. This discovery came as no surprise to the archaeological team; after all, they were digging inside a church. They carefully covered the remains and carried on, trying

Grey Friars church, Leicester. When the dig began in August 2012, the likelihood of discovering Richard's body was thought to be very slim indeed. It was anticipated that burials may be found but on the very first day, excavations uncovered the king's leg bones, although their significance was not understood until later, when the location of the choir had been established. (Courtesy of Snapper)

to establish the extent and orientation of the Friary and waiting for the arrival of the exhumation licence. No one suspected that this was, in fact, the skeleton of Richard III. They had hit lucky on their very first day.

Further discoveries followed. Using the glazed floor tiles, robbed-out walls and fragments of stained glass, the archaeologists established the location of the Grey Friars church. The presence of two stone benches with curved edges and separated by floor tiles suggested they had found the chapter house, where monks could sit and talk facing each other. Also, other remains were found, including a huge stone coffin, which looked to date from the thirteenth or fourteenth century. It clearly denoted a high-status burial and was starkly in contrast to Richard's final resting place. Excavated further in 2013, it is thought to contain the remains of either Peter Swynsfeld (d. 1272) or William of Nottingham (d. 1330), founders of the establishment. The other possibility is a burial that is known to have taken place in the church, that of Sir William Moton, who died in 1362. The stone sarcophagus revealed a lead coffin inside, which bore no identifying features to allow the archaeologists to make a definite identification.

Grey Friars trench, Leicester. Richard was buried in the choir of the church, which was located by the 2012 dig by using old maps of the location. The public were invited to observe the site on a number of locations but for the remainder of the time, it was protected from the gaze of spectators. This was especially important during the recovery of the bones from the trench. (Courtesy of Snapper)

The burial site of Richard III. The king had been buried in a small space, with his head and shoulders propped up. His hands were still tied and he does not appear to have been given a coffin, shroud or any grave goods. By contrast, an earlier individual buried in the church had been lain to rest in a lead coffin inside a stone sarcophagus. (Courtesy of Snapper)

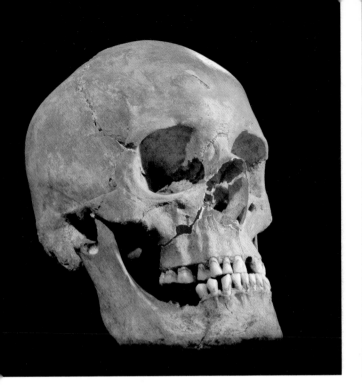

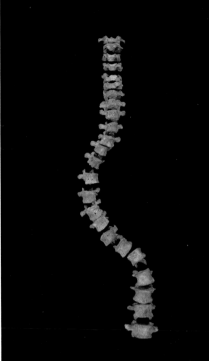

Above left: Skull of Richard III. Image released before press conference on 4 February 2013. (© University of Leicester)

Above right: Spine of Richard III. Richard's spine, excavated in September 2012, shows signs of idiopathic adolescent onset scoliosis, forming the distinctive 'S' shape, which would have caused some discomfort. (© University of Leicester)

Below: Skeleton of Richard III. The skeleton, minus feet, of Richard III, unveiled at the press conference of 4 February 2013. (© University of Leicester)

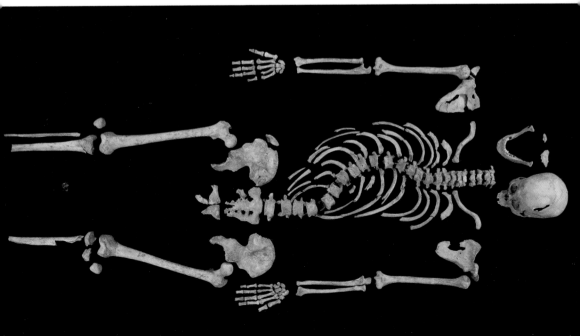

On 3 September 2012, the Ministry of Justice granted a licence 'for the removal of the remains of persons unknown'.[2] This must be 'effected with due care and attention to decency', the site must be screened from public view, and after exhumation, it must be kept 'safely, privately and decently' by the University of Leicester. Dr Jo Appleby and Dr Turi King donned protective suits to prevent the contamination of the remains, before climbing down into the trench and beginning the slow painstaking process of cleaning and lifting the bones. The following day, as the arms and ribcage were being cleared, the location of a window established that the remains were buried within the choir. Suddenly, the likelihood of them belonging to Richard became more real. A skull was uncovered, sitting above where the skeleton was anticipated to be lying, bearing the signs of trauma. Then, as Dr Appleby dug deeper, the spine emerged, clearly bent into an 'S' shape. The king had been found.

Or rather, most of him had. Save for his feet and a lower left leg bone, which were disturbed by Victorian building works, and a few small hand bones and teeth, the skeleton was intact. Incredibly, it had lain almost completely undisturbed only 680 millimetres below the surface of the car park. Very carefully, on the evening of 5 September 2012, what remained of the last Plantagenet king was lifted from his impromptu grave and placed in a cardboard box. These were draped with Richard's banner and driven away.

At Leicester University, a number of forensic examinations were made of the bones. The teeth indicated they had belonged to an individual who died in their late twenties to early thirties, consistent with Richard's age of thirty-two years at the time of his death. The angle of curve to the spine, clearly visible in the grave, was the result of idiopathic adolescent onset scoliosis. This meant it had no known cause and would have developed after the age of ten, probably when he went through the changes of puberty. Without it, he would have stood at around 5 feet 8 inches tall, but with the curve, his height was realistically more like 5 feet 4. The angle of the curve lay between 60 and 80 degrees but his condition may not have been visible beneath his clothes and he would have appeared normal as he walked. It may have caused some pain though, possibly placing additional pressure on his lungs and leading to shortness of breath. A further result of this was the unevenness of the shoulders, as the right clavicle was less worn than the left. The skeleton's arms were normal but unusually slender or gracile, and this, along with the wide pelvis, initially led the team to wonder if they were working with female remains.[3]

Samples carefully taken from the rib bones had been cross-checked in Glasgow and Oxford. Initially, the carbon dating indicated a date of death for the skeleton somewhere between 1430 and 1460. Richard had been born in 1452 but did not die until twenty-five years after this final estimate. However, the results indicated that the individual had enjoyed a diet rich in protein, particularly marine creatures, consistent with an upper-class lifestyle, which could provide variety and luxury even on the regular fast days in the Catholic calendar. This meant that the results needed to be adjusted, moving the date of death backwards in time, leaving a 95 per cent probability of a date between 1450 and 1540.[4]

Experts in medieval warfare worked closely with the university pathologists to examine the wounds to the skeleton. Ten separate wounds had been identified on the bones, two of which, to the skull, would have proved fatal. The first of these was a large hole at the back of the skull, caused by a large, sharp blade, perhaps a halberd, wielded with considerable pressure. A similar weapon had made the stab wound at the right-hand side of the skull, and penetrated more than 10 centimetres. Either of these would have been sufficient to kill Richard, but he also bore signs of further wounds, consistent with a sustained final attack. A flat blade had sliced at his skull in three places, at the back left and on the top, then a sharp point had been thrust into his crown, causing the skull to split and leaving two flaps of bone. This may have been caused by a dagger, like a further wound which pierced his cheek. Finally, the right side of his chin had been sliced into with a blade. None of these injuries would have been possible had Richard been wearing a helmet at the time, suggesting that he lost it along with his crown in his final moments in the marsh. There was a further cut to his ribs and pelvis, which may have been inflicted after death. He may also have suffered other injuries that left no mark upon his bones.[5]

The DNA results confirmed that there was a match between the bones and Richard's living relative, Michael Ibsen. This was the last piece in the jigsaw. Not only did the two men share a mitochondrial genetic code, they were also carriers of a rare genetic subgroup. It had been difficult to isolate and work with the delicate samples, taken from four molars found still *in situ* in the skull.[6] The chances of the material surviving and providing the required evidence, let alone a modern match, seemed slender at the least. Yet, almost like a fairy tale from start to finish, Richard had been located, found and identified. A facial reconstruction was also carried out, with a 3D scan of the skull sent to Professor Caroline Wilkinson at Glasgow University. The result was an impression that did not differ too wildly from the surviving portraits from the early sixteenth century. Incredibly, it became possible to look upon the face of England's last medieval king, killed in battle 527 years before. On Monday 4 February, a press conference in the city's Guildhall revealed the news to the world.

9

Reburial: 2013–2014

The dig might have been over, but the battle was just beginning. Although the university had planned for the reburial of any human remains before the diggers even lifted the tarmac, they had not expected they would be so lucky to find Richard himself. After the news of their discovery spread, with the details of the hurried grave at Grey Friars and humiliation wounds, questions surfaced about the nature and location of his reburial. All were in agreement that as a King of England, he deserved an honourable and respectful service and tomb. Some suggested this should take place at York Minster, instead of in Leicester Cathedral, which had been the original plan. The proposed schedule for reburial had offered a date for the ceremony in May 2014, but as a result of the legal wranglings that followed, it became necessary to use the full extent of the exhumation licence, which required interment to take place within two years, so before the end of August 2014. In the euphoria surrounding the unexpected discovery of his bones, no one could have predicted that Richard's remains would spark something of a modern-day Wars of the Roses.

Three options have been put forward for the reburial of Richard's bones: Westminster Abbey, Leicester Cathedral and York Cathedral. Although he had strong associations with other locations during his life, such as Middleham Castle, Ludlow Castle and Sheriff Hutton Castle, none of these have been considered suitable resting places for an English king.

Westminster Abbey, at the heart of government, has been the favoured location for the burial of royalty since before the Norman Conquest. Dedicated to the Anglo-Saxon St Erkenwald, London's saint, and then St Peter and Edward the Confessor, it has witnessed more key events in English history than any other building. Every monarch has been crowned there since 1066. Richard's wife, Anne, lies buried somewhere near the south ambulatory, where the Richard III Society erected a plaque in her name in 1960. Richard's nemesis, Henry VII, lies beside Elizabeth of York in the Lady Chapel he built and their granddaughters

A door at Leicester Cathedral, carved with a motif of roses. When the Grey Friars church was dismantled during the Reformation, many of the building materials were used to rebuild and extend St Martins, which was designated a cathedral in 1927. It had been catering to the souls of Leicester's people since Norman times. (Courtesy of Mike Cox)

Mary I and Elizabeth I are also interred nearby. Although others broke with tradition, like Edward IV choosing Windsor, Westminster would seem a natural choice for an English king. However, after 1,000 years of burials, the abbey is full. It simply cannot accommodate any more bodies. If Richard's bones were to be laid to rest there, they would need to be cremated first. For this reason, Westminster has been ruled out of the debate.

Leicester was an obvious choice because this was where Richard had originally been buried. In line with English Heritage's 2005 document regarding best osteoarchaeological practise, human remains are usually reinterred as close as possible to the place where they were found. The exhumation licence granted to the university on 3 September 2012 contained the condition that the remains must be 'deposited at Jewry Wall Museum or else be reinterred at St Martin's Cathedral or in a burial ground where interments may legally take place'.[1] In fact, this outcome had already been anticipated in the preliminary plans for the dig and as Richard clearly could not be returned to the car park, Leicester Cathedral was chosen as the most appropriate location. People have been worshipping on its site since Saxon times, with the first church being replaced by a Norman one, which was then developed during the medieval period. By the time Richard arrived in the city two days before Bosworth, St Martin's church was its main civic church, with strong links to the nearby Guildhall. There is also the nice touch of irony that after the dissolution, stones from the Grey Friars church were recycled to help extend St Martin's. It underwent further alterations and additions in Victorian times and was finally consecrated as a cathedral in 1927. In 1980, a slab in commemoration of Richard was unveiled in the chancel floor, which has provided a site for memorials since then. The strong public interest in the dig and its findings clearly required some sort of focus. A temporary exhibition opened in the Guildhall drew 80,000 visitors between February and June alone. A more permanent memorial is being planned though, with a £4 million visitor centre proposed for the city, which should attract 100,000 people annually. Named 'Richard III: Dynasty, Death and Discovery', it would be constructed near to the car park location and allow visitors to overlook a reconstruction of the medieval city.

However, a significant number of people have objected to Richard being buried at Leicester. This is founded on a number of reasons, including the belief that Richard had stronger associations elsewhere, that St Martin's Cathedral is not suitable and that it was the location of his ignominious previous burial. Some

The original slab commemorating Richard's death in Leicester Cathedral, long before the dig was planned, recognising his resting place in the long-lost Grey Friars church. It has been a site for Ricardian pilgrimage for many years. (Courtesy of Mike Cox)

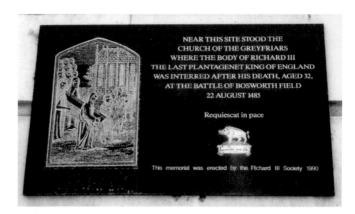

This plaque was placed by the Richard III Society in 1990, and marks the site of the Grey Friars church where Richard was buried. (Courtesy of David Baldwin)

The Guildhall, Leicester. Built around 1390 as a meeting place for the important Guild of Corpus Christi, it was used for the city corporation and would have been familiar to Richard during his visits. Later it was used as a library, courtroom and venue for drama. (Courtesy of Steve Cadman)

Until early in 2014, the Guildhall housed an exhibition of the Richard III dig, explaining the findings and the evidence that the bones belonged to Richard. It has seen record numbers of visitors. (Courtesy of Steve Cadman)

York's fifteenth-century Guildhall, seen from the River Ouse. Richard visited here on his royal progress in 1483. (Courtesy of David Baldwin)

went further to claim that it had been Richard's own intentions to be buried in York. Various challenges were mounted to the intended reburial, in the hope that the bones would be finally laid to rest in York Minster.

There had been a church at York since the fourth century, which gradually evolved into what is now one of the largest places of worship in Northern Europe. Significant work was undertaken during the fifteenth century, with the construction of two new towers and the rebuilding of the original one. It was consecrated as a cathedral during Richard's lifetime, in 1472; settling permanently at Middleham following his marriage that year, he may even have attended the ceremony, or at least visited soon after. In December 2012, between the discovery of Richard's remains and the news being made public, York welcomed the Very Reverend Vivienne Faull as its new dean, the first female dean in the history of Anglican Christianity. In an ironic twist of fate, before then, Dean Faull had been the Provost of Leicester Cathedral.

Richard was of the House of York and did visit the city many times, as he lived in Yorkshire. He also arranged for the investiture of his son as Prince of Wales to take place there in August 1483. However, although medieval surnames were originally allocated according to place and appearance, by this point in time they were independent of location, just as the Lancasters were not based in that county. The Wars of the Roses was a clash of two families and had little to do with geographical location. For the question of his burial, he must be considered as an English king rather than a representative of a region.

It has been claimed that Richard himself would have wanted to be buried in York but no evidence survives for this. No will was ever found, even if he had made one; after all, at the young age of thirty-two, he had not planned on losing the Battle of Bosworth. He may have founded chapels and left instructions for masses to be said in his name, but this is not an explicit declaration of intent. The plans that he made survive in the Fabric Rolls of York Minster, and include instructions for a college of 100 priests, with six altars, and a grant for those priests to sing in the minster.[2] However, this is similar to the establishment he intended to found at Middleham's Church of St Mary and Alkelda, as well as at Barnard Castle. If the numbers involved are larger in the York Rolls, this simply reflects the relative size of the cathedral in relation to the churches. No reference was made in Richard's plans to a tomb or chantry chapel.

Nor can a case be made that Richard's aims for York mirror his brother's founding of St George's Chapel at Windsor. Edward purposefully established a mausoleum, which stands out as a declaration of intention, rather than being typical of a pattern in his religious patronage. Richard did not live long enough to be able to demonstrate a further plan for the founding of collegiate churches as king, although he may well have gone on to do so. The fact that his instructions for York were so similar to the provision made for Middleham and Barnard Castle disproves any special intention for the minster. His actions do provide evidence of the fulfilment of his pious nature, his personal and regal duties, but they do not constitute evidence of his desire to be buried at York. Rather, as an anointed king, he would have anticipated burial in Westminster Abbey. He did not have the hindsight to know that he would die on the battlefield; in all eventualities he would have hoped to die peacefully in his bed and be laid to rest beside Anne.

A group was formed by Richard's distant relatives, the collateral descendants who are directly related to his siblings, with the intention of challenging the proposed Leicester reburial. Taking the name The Plantagenet Alliance, they launched a legal challenge, claimed that it was Richard's wish to be buried in York and that they had a right to have a say in the decision. An online petition failed to raise the required 100,000 signatures in order to request a Parliamentary debate on the topic. In fact, the subject had already been raised that March, when questions were raised during Member's Question Time by York MPs Hugh Bayley and Julian Sturdy. Responding to the strength of public feeling, they expressed their constituents' desire for a review. When the Alliance was formed, some time later, a spokesperson

Above: York Minster. The city of York and its cathedral were familiar to Richard during his lifetime; he also had plans to found a chantry there, where regular prayers would be said for him. After the discovery of his bones, calls have been made for his reburial here instead of at Leicester, in line with the original exhumation licence. (Courtesy of Paul Fairbrass)

Below left: A thirteenth-century stained-glass window in the cathedral at York; just one aspect of the location that Richard himself would have seen during his lifetime which still survives intact. (Courtesy of Steve Cadman)

Below right: These impressive stalls in York cathedral were carved during the nineteenth century but are in keeping with the Gothic style that Richard would have known. They dominate with their awe-inspiring scale and detail. (Courtesy of Steve Cadman)

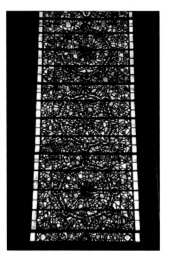

echoed this, claiming they had been forced into taking action, as the Leicester team had not realistically anticipated the discovery of a King of England, with all the historical significance that held for the country. They argued that it was a question to be decided by heads of state, or the nation itself, rather than a university.

In September 2013, the Alliance succeeded in securing a judicial review of the reburial plans, granted by a High Court judge, putting the arrangements of Leicester Cathedral on hold. A counter petition was launched by supporters of the original plan, and others have cited estimates that, in fact, anywhere between 1 and 17 million people are related to Richard III in the same degree as the collateral descendents.[3] This has caused many to question the Alliance's claim that they are the only people who can speak on behalf of Richard and that they 'know what he wanted'.[4] Only weeks later, though, it emerged that the Ministry of Justice was working with lawyers to overturn the review. The Justice Secretary, Chris Grayling, took the view that the system of judicial reviewing was not intended for such a case and that it was a waste of taxpayers' money. He stated that he would 'vigorously defend' the reburial of Richard in Leicester. The issue was also raised of the Alliance having waited eight months to launch their challenge, when the burial plans had been known since the king's discovery.[5] At the time of writing, the High Court's initial hearing is expected daily.

The question of the tomb also proved contentious. After the Richard III Society raised money for a suitable monument to be built, various designs were put forward. In September 2013, pictures of a proposed new tomb were unveiled, immediately sparking a storm of debate. Costing £1.3 million, they involved a complete reworking of the chantry at St Martin's, which cathedral officials described as 'the right place and the best place'.[6] In these images, the raised limestone block, tilted slightly to suggest resurrection and graved with a deep cross, sits atop a white York rose, enclosed by a black circle. At once it was dismissed by Philippa Langley and others as too modern and unfit for a 'medieval warrior King'.[7] Although the chairman of the Richard III Society described the design as 'inspired', many members who had contributed to the £40,000 raised for its construction contacted Langley to request their money be returned. Leicester Cathedral responded that it understood the concerns raised but could not be 'held hostage' for the money.[8] The design had already been altered once, after initial plans to lay the king under a flat slab had been met with similar resistance.

At the time of writing, these disputes have yet to be resolved. While no one has the ownership of Richard's bones, he has incited an unprecedented level of debate regarding the legal, moral and religious entitlement of such a high-status

Above: The Richard III tomb, designed by architects van Heyningen and Haward. (Courtesy of Leicester Cathedral, © van Heyningen and Haward)

Below: An interpretation of the view of the tomb from the choir. (Courtesy of Leicester Cathedral, © van Heyningen and Haward)

How the tomb would look in Leicester Cathedral. (Courtesy of Leicester Cathedral, © van Heyningen and Haward)

individual. These events have also redefined the relationship between people of the past and present, one over which Richard has no control. In life, he was the repository of divine and secular authority, who successfully suppressed many of the dissenting voices of his time and removed obstacles to his rule. As a medieval king, he aimed to curb conflict in his realm and accepted the throne in order to prevent a return to the factional rule that had torn the country apart for a previous generation. How ironic then, that his return from the dead should again force England into division.

Richard's prayer book was passed on to Margaret Beaufort after being discovered among his battle train. Today it resides in Lambeth Palace Library and includes this prayer, which he had adapted for his personal use:

Lord Jesus Christ, deign to free me, your servant King Richard, from every tribulation, sorrow and trouble in which I am placed ... hear me, in the name of all your goodness, for which I give thanks, and for all the gifts granted to me, because you made me from nothing and redeemed me out of your bounteous love and pity from eternal damnation to promising eternal life.[9]

Acknowledgements

Thanks go to the team at Amberley: Jonathan Reeve for suggesting this book and Nicola, Christian, Nicki and Alice for their continuing support and promotion. I have also been particularly lucky to have made some wonderfully helpful and knowledgeable friends online, who have generously shared their thoughts and time with me, in particular the members of my Edward IV discussion group. Thanks also to all my family, to my husband Tom for his love and support; also the Hunts, for Sue's generosity and John's local knowledge and continual supply of interesting and unusual books. Many thanks to Paul Fairbrass for his support, research and for driving about the country taking photographs. Most of all, this book is for my mother for her invaluable proofreading skills and for my father for his enthusiasm. This is the result of the books they read me, the museums they took me to as a child and the love and imagination with which they encouraged me.

Notes

Prologue

1. This is a fictional account of Richard's burial.

Introduction

1. Schama, Simon, 'Richard III, A King in Machiavellian Mode', *Financial Times*, 8 February 2013.

1 Richard Liveth Yet: 1452–1461

1. Wilkinson, Josephine, *Richard III, The Young King to Be* (Amberley, 2009).
2. More, Thomas.
3. Shakespeare, William, *Richard III*.

2 Royal Duke: 1461–1483

1. Bryner, Jeanna, 'Did Richard III Undergo Painful Scoliosis Treatment?', *LiveScience*, 19 April 2013.

2. Payne Collier, J. (ed.), *The Ghost of Richard III*, 1614 (London: Shakespeare Society, 1844).
3. Buck.
4. Ross, Charles, *Richard III* (University of California Press, 1981).

3 Princes in the Tower: 1483

1. Bentley, Samuel (ed.), *Excerpta Historica* (London, 1831).
2. Croyland Chronicle.
3. Fabyan, Robert, *The Concordaunce of Hystoryes*, 1516.
4. Cheetham, Anthony, *The Life and Times of Richard III* (Weidenfeld & Nicolson, 1972).
5. Cunningham, Sean, *Richard III, A Royal Engima* (The National Archives, 2003).
6. Lamb, V. B., *The Betrayal of Richard III: An Introduction to the Controversy* (Sutton, 1990,

first published 1959).
7. Mancini.
8. Jenkins, Elizabeth, *The Princes in the Tower* (Hamish Hamilton, 1978).

4   King: 1483–1485

1. Letter to the Mayor of York from Richard's secretary John Kendall, quoted in Cunningham.
2. Croyland.
3. Jenkins.
4. Croyland.
5. *Ibid.*
6. *Ibid.*
7. Jenkins.
8. Titulus Regis, extract in Cunningham.
9. Hicks, Michael, *Richard III* (Tempus, 1991).

5   Henry Tudor: 1457–1485

1. de Lisle, Leanda, *Tudor* (Chatto & Windus: 2013)
2. *Ibid.*
3. Crawford, Anne, *The Yorkists: The History of a Dynasty* (Continuum, 2007).
4. Holinshed.
5. de Lisle.

6   Bosworth: August 1485

1. Brereton, Nicholas, *Ballad of Lady Bessiye*.
2. Holinshed.
3. Ingram, Mike, *Battle Story: Bosworth 1485* (The History Press/Spellmount, 2012).
4. Fabyan.
5. Brereton.
6. Holinshed.
7. Langley, Philippa and Michael Jones.
8. Ingram.
9. McKinley, R. A., 'The City of Leicester: Political and Administrative History, 1066–1509', *A History of the County of Leicester: Volume 4: The City of Leicester* (1958), pp. 1–30.
10. Hoskins, W. G., *A History of the County of Leicestershire* (Victoria County Histories BHO).
11. Holinshed.
12. Langley and Jones.
13. Ingram.
14. *Ibid.*
15. *Ibid.*
16. Skidmore
17. *Ibid.*
18. Vergil
19. Ingram

7   Aftermath: 1485–2012

1. Hutton, William, *The Battle of Bosworth Field Between Richard III and Henry Earl of Richmond* (Pearson and Rollason, 1788).
2. Ingram.
3. Hutton.
4. Ingram.
5. Crawford.
6. Baldwin, David, 'King Richard's Grave in Leicester' (1986).
7. Schwyzer.
8. *Ibid.*
9. *Ibid.*
10. *Ibid.*
11. Buck, George, *A History of King Richard III* (London, W. Wilson, 1674).
12. SLP 'Henry VIII', 10 November 1538, p. 791.
13. Jones and Langley.
14. Schwyzer.
15. Lamb.
16. *Ibid.*
17. Schama.

8   Investigation: 2011–2013

1. Baldwin
2. Exhumation Licence, http://www.le.ac.uk/richardiii/documents/Licence.pdf
3. http://www.le.ac.uk/richardiii/index.html, plus my notes taken while watching the *King in the Car Park* documentary on 4/2/13.
4. *Ibid.*
5. *Ibid.*
6. *Ibid.*

9   Reburial: 2013–2014

1. Exhumation Licence.
2. Hammond, P. W., 'Richard III and York', *Ricardian Bulletin* (December 2012), pp. 50–1.
3. Taylor, Emily, 'Identifying Richard III; An Interview with Dr Turi King', *The Post Hole*, http://theposthole.org/read/article/216.
4. Vanessa Roe, interview with the BBC, 12/9/13.
5. Pocklington, David, *Richard III Reburial: Ministry of Justice to Challenge Decision for Judicial Review?* lawandreligionuk.com, 12/10/13.
6. BBC News, 22/9/13.
7. BBC News, 23/9/13.
8. *Ibid.*
9. Leicester Cathedral Website, http://www.cathedral.leicester.anglican.org/Visit%20&%20support%20us/RichardIII.html

Bibliography

Ashdown-Hill, John, *Eleanor, the Secret Queen: The Woman Who put Richard III on the Throne* (The History Press, 2009).

Ashdown-Hill, John, *The Last Days of Richard III and the Fate of His DNA: The Book that Inspired the Dig* (The History Press, reprint 2013).

Baldwin, David, *Elizabeth Woodville* (The History Press, new ed. 2004).

Baldwin, David, 'King Richard's Grave in Leicester' (1986 paper, http://www.le.ac.uk/lahs/downloads/BaldwinSmPagesfromvolumeLX-5.pdf).

Baldwin, David, *Richard III* (Amberley, 2012).

Bentley, Samuel (ed.), *Excerpta Historica* (London, 1831).

Bird, W. H. B. and K. H. Ledward (eds), *Calendar of State Papers, Henry VI, Edward IV, Edward V, Richard III* (1953).

Brereton, Nicholas, *The Ballad of Lady Bessiye* (http://newr3.dreamhosters.com/wp-content/uploads/2013/02/ladye_bessiye.pdf).

Bryner, Jeanna, 'Did Richard III Undergo Painful Scoliosis Treatment?', *LiveScience* (19 April 2013).

Buck, George, *A History of King Richard III* (London: W. Wilson, 1674).

Carson, Annette, *Richard III: A Small Guide to the Great Debate* (2013).

Cheetham, Anthony, *The Life and Times of Richard III* (Weidenfeld & Nicolson, 1972).

Crawford, Anne, *The Yorkists: The History of a Dynasty* (Continuum, 2007).

Cunningham, Sean, *Richard III, A Royal Engima* (The National Archives, 2003).

de Lisle, Leanda, *Tudor* (Chatto & Windus, 2013).

Dobson, R. B., 'Richard III and the Church of York' in R. A. Griffiths and J. Sherborne (eds), *Kings and Nobles in the Late Middle Ages* (Gloucester, 1986).

Ellis, Henry (ed.), *New Chronicles of England and France in two parts by Robert Fabyan, 1516* (London, 1811).

Ellis, Henry (ed.), *Three Books of Polydore Vergil's English History, comprising the reigns of Henry VI, Edward IV and Richard III* (Camden Society, 1844).

Gairdner, James (ed.), *Gregory's Chronicle 1461-9* (London, 1876).

Gregory, Philippa, David Baldwin and Michael Jones, *The Women of the Cousins' War: The Duchess, the Queen and the King's Mother* (Simon & Schuster, 2011).

Hall, Edward, *Chronicle; containing the History of England, during the reign of Henry the fourth and the succeeding monarchs, to the end of the reign of Henry VIII, in which are particularly described the manners and customs of those periods* (Collated with the editions of 1548 and 1550) (London: J. Johnson, 1809).

Hammond, P. W., 'Richard III and York', *Ricardian Bulletin* (December 2012, 50-1).

Hammond, P. W. and Anne F. Sutton, *Richard III: The Road to Bosworth Field* (Constable, 1985).

Hancock, Peter A., *Richard III and the Murder in the Tower* (The History Press, 2011).

Hicks, Michael, *Anne Neville* (Tempus, 2007).

Hicks, Michael, *Edward V: The Prince in the Tower* (Tempus, 2003).

Hicks, Michael, *Richard III* (Tempus, 2000).

Holinshed, Raphael, *Chronicles of England, Scotland and Ireland* (London: J. Johnson, 1807).

Hoskins, W. G., *A History of the County of Leicestershire* (Victoria County Histories, BHO).

Hutton, William, *The Battle of Bosworth Field Between Richard III and Henry Earl of Richmond* (Pearson and Rollason, 1788).

Ingram, Mike, *Battle Story: Bosworth 1485* (The History Press/Spellmount, 2012).

Jenkins, Elizabeth, *The Princes in the Tower* (Hamish Hamilton, 1978).

Kendall, Paul Murray, *Richard III* (W. W. Norton & Co., 1955).

Lamb, V. B., *The Betrayal of Richard III: An Introduction to the Controversy* (Sutton, 1990), (first published 1959).

Langley, Philippa and Michael Jones, *Richard III: The Search for Richard III: The King's Grave* (John Murray, 2013).

Licence, Amy, *Anne Neville: Richard III's Tragic Queen* (Amberley, 2012).

Mancini, *The Occupation of the Throne by Richard III* (1483).

McKinley, R. A., 'The City of Leicester: Political and administrative history, 1066–1509', *A History of the County of Leicester: Volume 4: The City of Leicester* (BHO, 1958).

More, T., *The History of King Richard III*, ed. J. Rawson Lumby (Cambridge University Press, 1883).

Payne Collier, J. (ed.), *The Ghost of Richard III*, 1614 (London: Shakespeare Society, 1844).

Penn, Thomas, *The Winter King: The Dawn of Tudor England* (Allen Lane, 2011).

Petre, J. (ed.), *Richard III: Crown and People, A Selection of Articles from The Ricardian Journal of the Richard III Society, March 1975 to December 1981* (Alan Sutton, 1985).

Pollard, A. J., *Richard III and the Princes in the Tower* (Alan Sutton, 1991).

Riley, Henry T. (trans.), *Ingulph's Chronicle of the Abbey of Croyland* (London: H. G. Bohn, 1854).

Ross, Charles, *Richard III* (University of California Press, 1981).

Rous, John. *This Rol was Laburd and finished by Master John Rows of Wararrewyk* (London: William Pickering, 1848).

Rymer, Thomas, *Foedera*, 1704–1735 (British History Online).

Saul, Nigel, *The Three Richards: Richard I, Richard II and Richard III* (Hambledon and London, 2005).

Schama, Simon, 'Richard III, A King in Machiavellian Mode', *Financial Times* (8 February 2013).

Schwyzer, Philip, *Shakespeare and the Remains of Richard III's Tomb* (Oxford University Press, 2013).

Seward, Desmond, *The Wars of the Roses* (Constable & Co., 1995).

Shakespeare, William, *Richard III*, ed. John Jowett (Oxford World's Classics, 2000).

Skidmore, Chris, *Bosworth* (Weidenfeld & Nicolson, 2013).

Sutton, Anne F. and Livia Visser-Fuchs '"Richard Liveth Yet": An Old Myth', *Ricardian* (June 1992).

Taylor, Emily, 'Identifying Richard III; An Interview with Dr Turi King', *The Post Hole* (http://theposthole.org/read/article/216).

Walpole, H., *Historic Doubts on the Life and Reign of Richard III* (1768).

Weir, Alison, *Lancaster and York: The Wars of the Roses* (Vintage, 1995).

Weir, Alison, *The Princes in the Tower* (Vintage, 1992).

Wilkinson, Josephine, *Richard III, The Young King to Be* (Amberley, 2009).

Richard III from Amberley Publishing

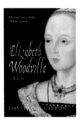

RICHARD III
David Baldwin

'A believably complex Richard, neither wholly villain nor hero'
PHILIPPA GREGORY

£9.99   978-1-4456-1591-2   272 pages PB 81 illus, 57 col

ANNE NEVILLE
Amy Licence

'Timely ... the real life of the daughter of Warwick the Kingmaker'
WI LIFE

£20.00   978-1-4456-1153-2   224 pages HB 30 illus, 10 col

ELIZABETH WOODVILLE
David MacGibbon

£20.00   978-1-4456-1275-1   256 pages HB 30 illus, 15 col

THE PRINCES IN THE TOWER
Josephine Wilkinson

£18.99   978-1-4456-1974-3   192 pages HB

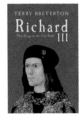

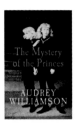

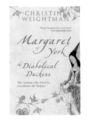

RICHARD III
Terry Breverton

£16.99   978-1-4456-2105-0   200 pages HB 20 col illus

RICHARD III: THE YOUNG KING TO BE
Josephine Wilkinson

£9.99   978-1-84868-513-0   352 pages PB 40 illus, 25 col

THE MYSTERY OF THE PRINCES
Audrey Williamson

'Brilliant and readable'
THE TRIBUNE

£9.99   978-1-84868-321-1   192 pages PB 40 col illus

MARGARET OF YORK
Christine Weightman

'Brings Margaret alive once more'
THE YORKSHIRE POST

£10.99   978-1-4456-0819-8   256 pages PB 51 illus

FORTHCOMING

Michael Hicks, *THE FAMILY OF RICHARD III*
Susan Fern, *THE MAN WHO KILLED RICHARD III*
Amy Licence, *CECILY NEVILLE*

ALSO AVAILABLE AS EBOOKS
Available from all good bookshops or to order direct
Please call **01453-847-800**
www.amberleybooks.com